SCHOOL MANAGEMENT THOUGHTS

DR DHEERAJ MEHROTRA

Contents

Preface

School Management Thoughts is a collection of quotes and references towards effective school management and its strategies with the march of time. Post Corona, the activation of learning has yielded yet another challenge to manage a school. We as educators look forward to effective management of teaching, learning and running the school with the priorities on our table. For sure the activation desire the leading of the school towards development through not only the optimum use of the human resources, physical sources, principles and concepts that help in achieving all the objectives of the school but also the proper coordination and adjustment among all of them.

Happy Reading Guys!

Dr Dheeraj Mehrotra

CHAPTER ONE

The Management of a School

Being a head of a school myself, I feel managing the students, teachers and above all the parents takes a significant toll towards the satisfaction which has to in any case prevail. The ultimate is that there is no practical training available for the Principals to manage the school. Whatsoever is the experience, over the years of teaching and learning that the individuals look forward to delivering and practice.

The facts reveal that the ultimate is the recap that the people tend to reflect for a better outcome. Here are some of the Thoughts on School Management that appear to be the saviour to the majority towards excellence in education at large.

CHAPTER TWO

School Management Thoughts

I walked along the road to retrace, wishfully thinking of a change to be for a chance to see academically, administratively holistically, technically, innovatively and above all humanely. There were many halts on the road traversed, with doubts, crisis, stress, timelines and variants of behaviours that needed analysis, deliberations, solutions through transparency, communications, associations among all stakeholders - parents teachers, top management and most relevant ones- the students. These revolve around the goals and vision with the enforcing mission as the hallmarks of managing the school. The Pedagogical strategies are the icing that completely adds to the impact of leadership in transacting school management realising it gradually"- **Dr Prerna Mitra, Principal, Army Public School, Bangalore**

CHAPTER THREE

Digital Skills For Teachers

A Teacher, who is now a FACILITATOR in this generation encapsulates a new order of delivery with the extension of a knowledge society and not a content delivery or an interpretation of book knowledge in real life. Innovation is the ultimate to generate interest in learning for the kids today. It mounts a lot of energy and thoughts to be an innovative educator who is of certain requirements to deliver the knowledge to the cyber society of today.

The mantra is Engage Me or Enrage Me, from the side of the students at large. As a matter of fact, it is true to the world that the teachers are no longer the sole imparters of knowledge but they need to empower the students to learn at the pace and at their leisure through personal learning networks keeping their special traits of talents and interests. The teachers just don't end up after the class is over but on the jolt for 24 hours around the cyber linkage or social networks further. There is no wall now or the boundary of learning. The innovative educator has to evolve a personal learning network for his or her improvement first. Not only this, it has to reach the students as well wherein there is no boundary of limitation in a big way. It is a way to build ones' own classroom and one's own network of learning. The change or the shift here is that we can connect around and share ideas that are not so in the one to many modes of classroom learning. The new age imaginative teacher has to be fertile in laminating the knowledge from roots and share the same with his students of all ages and figures. It also reflects off a Quality Teacher to share the unknown and the unnoticed with the religious sentiments of repute. We are on the look of an age where the teachers are at ease to conduct the assemblies online with students at distance apart to bring connection and pace of learning to happen in reality. The objective has to be TEACHERS substituting GOOGLE.

The fact lies in the Teacher being an Innovator of traits and essence to explore the attention in the classroom. The priority of taking Education and technology as a means to go together and it laminates with the questions in our minds viz.

Should we do more, less? What about virtual

schools? Interactive whiteboards? Cell phones? Facebook and Twitter? Should we let kids be out there on the 'net? Should we post their pictures? These are legitimate conversations, and each person has to make these kinds of decisions based on their own comfort levels and according to the needs of the individual child. To my knowledge and interest, they must be given an opportunity only when required but as a habit. From expertise gained from Facebook to Twitter, From blogs to scribing and skyping to celebrating ORM (Online Reputation Management) to explore is a necessity to engage in classrooms 24x7.

The innovative learning is not limited to a physical space but an open learning scenario with a preface to one's comfort at his reading home at home or a TV room at large. It is very much unlike the classroom learning with the same group all days, all the time. Here the community is different and the learning is more spectacular further. Here the teacher concerned is the one who has to be engaged and involved in the conversations as a leader or a facilitator further.

What is a priority for the Educators, policymakers and the private sector is the need to strive together and make India a global superpower by 2020. The five year plans in India root to new phases at times but the delivery is hard to explode in particular.

As per the demands and research, the challenge is to create an integrated education system that:

Provides access to quality education that is practical, relevant, customised and effective

Can adopt innovative ways (tech-based) to provide faster expansion of opportunities of education to all

*Looks for bridging the gap between education and employability * Promotes social equality/ economic viability*

The priority on cards needs to have an updated broadband connection to the Internet in order to make it possible for growing schools to provide the Quality Base and Information of Learning with a comic effect which further details the information towards the liking of the children in particular. The emphasis is on the requirements which promote the Smart Learning Environment which offers the students and the staff access to all the resources, online storage and communications tools they could ever need - not just during the school day, but beyond it too. As a matter of fact, further, the New technologies go way beyond paper-and-pencil to enable children to express themselves textually, graphically, numerically, aurally or visually but also to allow children to discover new ways to collaborate and learn. As a matter to observe and ponder over, in a national survey, teachers say they believe that using digital games in the classroom helps students maintain concentration and enthusiasm for learning, while making it easier for teachers to differentiate instruction and assess students.

As we are not well outdated and unreferenced with the tab that Digital natives and digital immigrants are terms coined by the American futurist Marc Prensky to distinguish between those who have grown up with technology and those who have adapted to it, there is an urgent need and analysis of when and how we need to change ourselves to the existing scenario and get to the bargain price of Changing with the environment and the opportune moment otherwise. There is a heavy need for perfection bound to produce our existence otherwise with a tag of Old Generation buddies otherwise like that of a civilization hence.

The requirements in addition, as we know of observation, the overall, learning today is much more interactive than it used to be. On-demand, the very Learning has had become significantly richer as students have access to new and different types of information, they can manipulate it on the computer through graphic displays or controlled experiments in ways never before possible, and they can communicate the results of their efforts to teachers through a variety of media. We need to involve them, make them a learning partner and above all explore their creativity further. New ways of obtaining and presenting information have given students powerful new ways of analysing and understanding the world around them, and research also shows that children who use technology to support their learning are more motivated and engaged.

With clarity and congestion, practically, Education is increasingly infused with media content, which can distract students by leading them into too many conflicting directions at once, discouraging their commitment to any one path. Teaching ethics and international relations in the classroom without borders is a commitment to our growth as human beings in a world in desperate need of humanity during a time of moral crisis.

Classrooms today are more diverse than ever before. The same cannot be said about textbooks, curriculum, and lesson plans. Teachers must design lessons that are accessible to all students and reflect their diversities. One has to as well, explore different approaches to traditional learning systems and find out how to implement new strategies to engage students in lessons. The teachers of the new age of Demand and Liking need to be open to ADAPTING, Being Visionary towards perfection, Collaborating of choice and energy with sharing of routine operations towards betterment at ease and fraternity keeping the audience in mind. He or she needs to be having modelling behaviour, must be leading, open to taking risks and above all keen to learn. In addition, the Quality Educator also models tolerance, global awareness and reflective practice, whether

it is the quiet, personal inspection of their teaching and learning process or through blogs, Twitter and others.

It is quite alarming to note and analyze the fact that, according to researchers we are in the midst of a sea change in the way that we read and think. Our digitally native children have wonderfully flexible minds. They absorb information quickly, adapt to changes and are adept at culling from multiple sources. But they are also suffering from internet-induced attention deficit disorder.

The quality culture today demands with perfection the art and artistic attitude of the teachers which in flash to make the best of efforts and pride culture within the classrooms in a big way. There is an urgent need to answer the google generation today and for this one has to be more INFORMED and calculated towards knowledge these days.

As an academician, I do feel that "Everyone is a genius. But, if you judge a fish by its ability to climb a tree, it will live its whole life believing that it is stupid." as do one of the inventors of past years. For every teacher today the task to manage the GOOGLE Generation is possible with the fragrance of TECH CANDIES as a priority. The teacher's bucket list of DIGITAL hunger of knowledge and expertise has to have on the go to explore. Kudos to the support from the school management who provide the best pace and infrastructure to nurture them on shelves.

Cheers and Happy Learning.....

CHAPTER FOUR

Integrating NLP in delivering Excellence

NLP- Integrates unleashing the power for success and happiness. Academics is just another kingdom to deliver the essence!

The Neuro-Linguistic Programming, the NLP derives the essence of learning via

Neuro: Which integrates the five senses, Visual, auditory, kinesthetic, olfactory and Gustatory. Visual includes Sights:: Auditory defines sounds we hear:: Kinesthetic defines external feelings like a touch of someone or something:: Olfactory means smell:: Gustatory means taste!

Linguistic: Defines the language and other nonverbal communication systems through which our neural representations are coded and include pictures, sounds, feelings, tastes, smells and words.

Programming: is an art to discover and utilize the instructions we run as our communication to ourselves and others to achieve our specific and desired outcomes. It is a tested and progressive model of how we communicate with ourselves and others. It was originally developed by Richard Bandler, John Grinder and others.

The productivity of individuals is explored to the best via the incentives generated of experience and target vision in particular.

In academics, as a novice spectrum, the NLP integrates into discovering the art of knowing the students with their level of acceptance and learning in totality. It is like how to use the language of the mind to consistently achieve our specific and desired outcomes to deliver the knowledge aimed at the students. Based on the teachers' experience in the classrooms, the exploring is delivered via the following:

Establishing rapport with an individual student which will enable you to help them better and create a win-win situation for everyone.

Have a rapport with the group of students by using pacing and leading. Use this to turn the entire group around to your agenda while remaining in charge.

Teaching students using the primary senses which entails determining the primary sense system of the student and then delivering information in a way that works best for that system.

Learning how to read students' minds by learning how to read their eye movements.

Exploring and identifying the balance between right brain days and left brain days.

Determining which mode the class is in and then teaching in a manner appropriate to the mood of the day in particular.

The subjective analysis within the classrooms attract effective communication skills by teachers and replicates them to the students at large. The concept integrates the language of the mind to consistently achieve our specific and desired outcomes. The education delivery with excellence after identifying the traits of the audience is hence an art being explored via this. This is indeed a great way to facilitate change. It allows us to be in a position wherein there is no concern or a problem. The mindset is a policy here to deliver the best. Some of the ratios which govern this aspect of curing intelligence by educators involve a push, getting out of the comfort zone, shy zone, arranging a massive paradigm shift, discussing the passion, learning to learn from the environment, must feel most alive, need to be happy in your own skin, give oneself a round of applause, empower the limiting belief and the negative emotions about self. Classroom teaching is a nourishing talent that crops with the march of time and tide. Behavioural flexibility narrates to the positive outcome only through the sensory acuity and psychology of excellence.

The teaching techniques need to excel with the 'wow' feature with a positive belief by the educators. The nurturing keys to an achievable outcome follow as:

Being positive

Specified present situation

Specified outcome

Specified evidence procedure

Self-initiated and self-maintained

Appropriately contextualized

Must be ecological

The approaches govern a practical approach to "All I need is within me now !", let the teachers approach students with a say "Raise your hand high and tall and say YES !" to promote the sense of agility and promptness during the sessions. The excellence which we point to activates with the six human needs for our students and the educators, in particular, the activation delivers via Certainty, Uncertainty/ Variety, Love & Connection, Significance, Growth and Contribution. All these replicate to confidence and deliver the power to perform. As teachers, we need to abide by the presuppositions of the NLP which act like convenient assumptions. It is a requisite of desire to respect for the other person's model of the world, the behaviour and change are to be evaluated in terms of context and Ecology. The resistance in a client (student) is a real sign of a lack of rapport. People (pupils) are not their behaviours, Everyone is doing the best one can with the resources they have available, every behaviour is motivated by positive intent. As a teacher, one has to calibrate on behaviour as the most important information about a person is that person's behaviour.

Mirroring in classrooms: *As teachers, the Mirroring technique of NLP distinguishes the matching portions of another person's behaviour, as in a mirror. This justifies the learning and the learner and the interest* *between them.*

Modelling with children: *This is another important technique to set the process of learning where we elicit the strategies, filter patterns and physiology that allows someone to produce a certain behaviour. This can be further tackled, modelled and paced as required.*

Pacing with Children: *This activates the conclusion. It delivers the matching or mirroring of another person's external behaviour so as to gain rapport. The joy with the kids encounter at ease and perforates learning as a resultant.*

The spectrum of learning for fun gets via this NLP which suffices to the limitations of dissatisfaction among the masses, particularly the stakeholders viz. the students and the parents. Activation of this would certainly result in penetration to learning as a habit rather than an occasional occurrence.

CHAPTER FIVE

Audits in Schools

Quality at the workplace has been an in thing of demand by the majority and its inception has been of repute by the Parents, the ultimate stakeholders including the students and the society at large. The particular conjunction to the need delivers a demand to pursue the quality learning environment which otherwise remains of the junction to a limit only.

The class organization and the opportunities to the children given within the classroom by the teachers really pertain to the existing norms and liking of the teachers at pace in particular. Also, the factors which influence the need for audit limit to planning for continuity and progression in learning, match of work to student's needs, interests and the clarity of objectives without which the tots do not feel at home within the four walls. Above all, the teaching tools in practice need to be evaluated with reference to the user during the lesson being appropriate or not. With this the teachers' subject knowledge, enthusiasm, methods of questioning, exposition and problem solving related to the multilevel dimension for judging. Also whether the work is tailored to individual needs or not is a concern for parents and the management of the school.

As rightly judged and defined by the researchers that Schools need to switch over from academic excellence to overall excellence. This can be done only if we re-engineer the human resources available with the teachers. They have to be retrained to the modern aspects of multimedia technology and the current thinking in education. The classrooms must be made centres of excellence.

It is required to judge the following factors in particular on priority:

Curriculum Planning

Teaching Learning Processes

Student Assessment and Performance

The Teaching-Learning Process forms the basis of the academic process and products. The need for Quality Assessment is a novel way by the Central Board of Secondary Education to pave the delivery in the best possible manner. It relates to the following objectives viz.

To assess and endorse that an institution/ school meets established standards.

To assess the effectiveness of an institution in creating the most innovative, relevant, socially conscious eco-oriented learning ambience for all its staff and students.

To involve the faculty comprehensively in institutional evaluation and planning for enhancing the effectiveness of a school.

To establish criteria for professional certification and upgrading of standards.

To encourage continuous self-assessment, accountability and autonomy in innovation in school education.

To encourage continuous professional development and capacity building of teachers.

This type of audit or assessment is intended to be a means to document the strengths and weaknesses of educational practices and institutional effectiveness leading them to the desired accountability towards the society and the stakeholders further. The process is bound to entertain issues related to the strengths of the school with areas of development, professional skills and upliftment required and the classroom management format of demand.

CHAPTER SIX

Mindfulness Within Classrooms

The present scenario of TECHNOLOGY ADOPTION in the learning spectrum of students tends to re-locate them to distractions in a big way. The majority of the students in the pace of the classroom towards their day dreaming with the molecules of PS4 and X-Box characters and Social Networking responses in expectations. The very aged generation has short attention spans and they have a lot of vying for our deliberations during the lessons in particular. The 'Happiness Curriculum' launched by the Delhi government focuses on holistic education by including meditation, value education, and mental exercises in the conventional education curriculum.

It has been introduced for the students of nursery to Class 8 in government schools from July 12. The new subject has been designed and prepared by a team of 40 Delhi government teachers, educators and volunteers over a period of six months. Here lies the MINDFULNESS wherein the present is owned by the students with the facilitators through the calming of the mind and increase awareness of their bodies, thoughts and emotions. The syntax of making them relaxed, centred and engaged is the inertia towards developing robust strategies for implementing mindfulness techniques within the classrooms.

Many people think that mindfulness is only beneficial for adults because it is only adults that can feel stress. But contrary to popular belief, stress can affect children as well, especially in school. Students experience toxic stress every single day due to pressure to get good grades, an increasingly competitive environment and also the uncertainty of the future. The happiness quotient re-invents the preface with productivity at large.

It is very common now to hear third-grade students say that they felt like dying when they failed to understand a subject in school or got bad grades. This is why teaching mindfulness in school is very important. It is an important method to help students cope with stress as well as achieve excellence in learning.

Improve Attention and Cognitive Skill

One of the biggest reasons why students can't focus in class is because of low attention span. Even straight-A students can lose focus every once in a while and it often makes them feel bad about themselves.

Mindfulness meditation can solve this problem because it directly affects the brain, especially the hippocampus part. Practising mindfulness can help the students to concentrate better. And since it jogs the hippocampus to be more active, their memory and critical learning skill will be improved and help them get better grades.

Develop Better Interpersonal Skill

The competition and also pressure to always be the best in class can affect the student's social and emotional skills. They tend to only focus on themselves and don't care about what's happening around them.

Interpersonal skill is very important to survive in the real world. So, the school must make sure that the pressure to perform well in school will not harm their interpersonal skill. Mindfulness training will also make the prefrontal cortex, the part of the brain that regulates emotion, more active. As a result, the students will be able to be more empathetic, more sociable as well as improve their behaviour in school.

Help Students Coping with Stress

Stress is not a stranger in human's life and it is also very normal for students to experience stress when facing a challenging time in their education. However, the situation of the modern education system often forces the students to experience toxic stress, the kind of stress that can negatively affect their mental health.

The worst thing about this is the fact that the majority of the students don't know how to deal with their stress. This is the most dangerous part of stress. Stress is normal, but if the students don't know how to cope with it, it will lead to various problems from an inability to regulate mood, impaired attention, even physical problems and depression.

School should not only focus on lessons and grades, but also education for life. The education system should really start to pay attention to the student's well being too, and mindfulness meditation is one of the best methods for that. It will teach the students to improve their mindful awareness that can help them cope with stress, improve their optimism about life and also improve their performance in school. The techniques herein fetch building up of the social and emotional skills of the children and foster students' academic performance by implementing cognitive practices which as a result develops their metacognitive skills and speaking in particular.

CHAPTER SEVEN

Knowledge Retention Within Classrooms

Wow, the activated classroom is a fun learning exploring for quality and satisfaction. How children learn is a concern today, for we can not teach how we were taught. Teaching through technology must be a practise rather than an occasional occurrence, for sure if there has to be a Wow feature within classrooms.

As teachers, we must not use technology as a silicon coating but harness the power of technology to connect with our students. No more, it is about copying and pasting, which we have had been doing over the years. Power corrupts politicians, so PowerPoint corrupts the teachers with just slides and no explanations. For a matter of thought and intelligence, the platform should share for show rather than expecting it to be the only parcel for knowledge delivery. There is a specific need to implement a new way of teaching through technology, and hence a digital pedagogy is required the most. The teachers need to introspect how children may learn in this networked environment. We can't simply take a textbook and deliver it digitally; somewhat the need here is to explore the power to harness the best via connectivity and creativity to connect.

We can't think and re-discover the chalkboard and make it a smartboard to deliver knowledge. What is required is a novel mindset of love, care and delivery of priorities for our children within classrooms. We ultimately need a different paradigm for teaching, a different pedagogy which talks about creation, control of chaos, connection to correcting and above all consumption to creation. The teachers need to change their thinking of how they are going to use technology in education.

For sure, we are living in a world of change, there are ample tweets each minute, ample facebook page views each minute. The academic Donald Norman describes skeuomorphism in terms of cultural constraints: interactions with a system that are learned only through culture. The term intensifies the tech world with pride. The world has only been used in the tech industry for a few years, where its meaning has changed, says Dan O'Hara, an academic at Birmingham City University. "Skeumorphs are not strictly something that can be designed," he says. "They occur unintentionally when aesthetic styles are inherited without thinking." The photo views of Flickr which mounts to n' undefined, explore the universal learning of repute. With each minute of over 47,000 app downloads on the apple store encapsulates a new phase of dimensional learning taking place out of the hunger for knowledge. Of course, all these facts did not exist before 2004 by any chance. The availability of data online fascinates the new learner in multiple ways who tend to be a multitasker in pave to grab the unknown. To sound far-fetched but true, the schools over the years have not changed. They have taken the same task to be limited to rows and columns with a teacher at pace. They typically at large have no technology hence there has been no change. There are reports too, "Failed iPad Experiment Shows BYOD Belongs in Schools.", "LA. Cancels iPads-in-the-schools program: a failure of vision, not technology. In spite of all our heavy investments at schools, it appears there is a failure of our strategy or the vision to implement the best of technology in education.

And above all, it appears the failure of our pedagogy. One of our mistakes as educators is CTRL + C & CTRL + V. Necessarily as COPY and PASTE for this just can't solve the concerns but expands the issue in particular. This is one of the mistakes we get to govern while implementing technology in our schools.

Similarly, the conclusion goes by fetching the scenario of obvious reasons, which relate to shifting the teaching into a new realm. The core teaching principles having a shift, need an @ctivated model so as to conclude with the no looking back in perfection. The teachers need to be an advocate for holistic education. This transforms the learners in a big way to assist learning and make it happen within the classrooms. Teachers need to keep things simple and do what works for them. For us, the teachers cannot teach the way we were taught. Above all the students, at large, would only like the subject if they like the teacher and this is one of the solitaire truths for any holy classroom in particular. Teachers need to have a wellness routine planning sheet, getting the win-win approach of the happiness index of the students, roll number wise. Indeed, classroom management has been identified as a major concern for teachers and if they don't get along with the learners as bosses or clients with affection, the management of the class appears slang. The teachers in the majority have a wrong notion that classroom management is much to do with discipline only and is limited to the children being quiet in the class, whereas the goals include identification of misconceptions about managing the teaching, the students and the consequences. The teachers of age need to broader the very conception of classroom management and ultimately need to provide a framework among the colleagues for developing their own classroom management plan. Engaging the children in instructions often leads to classroom management but is limited to a classic time only. For having an activated classroom, there has to be a thoughtful physical environment supported by establishing caring relationships and the implementation of engaging instructions.

CHAPTER EIGHT

The Learning Cycle: Post Pandemic!

Post CORONA, we aim at a new normal. Both at workplaces as well as schools, things and expectations have changed. To the range of Understanding, Mentor and the Instructor's overview is the most compelling concern for incompleteness. The cloud computer Circumstance triggers the connection with satisfaction to learn/ share/ work together and mix the understanding training overview within colleges.

Throughout the years, with the march of time and trend, the education and learning system has provided progression to the country and the globe as all Leading firms around the world focus and service the roles of Indians that are recognized for their Know-how and Knowledge.

To our satisfaction and excellence, the Indian Education and learning is honoured to the international education and learning globe for the INTENTION OF THE DECIMAL SYSTEM and the EXPLORATION OF NO. This stays our previous golden era of Education and learning teaching Circumstances.

The ingenious understanding is not restricted to a physical room; however, an open knowing circumstance with beginning to one's convenience at his checking outhouse in your home or a Television Room at big. It is significantly unlike the course space discovering with the same team all the time, at all times. Below the neighborhood is various as well as the knowledge is extra stunning better.

The knowing circumstance of upgrade needs a couple of required viz.

Supplying accessibility to high-quality education and learning that is functional, appropriate, personalized, and reliable.

Embrace ingenious methods (tech-based) to supply faster growth of chances of education and learning to all.

Discover linking the void in between teaching and learning and employability.

Advertise social equality/economic practicality.

These components the activation of innovation in the direction of High Getting results and recipient contentment amongst institutions.

When it comes to carrying out the brand-new devices of understanding, the promo has produced in creating the High-quality cult in colleges these days with a range of inputs with the stakeholders viz—moms and dads, Trainees, as well as educators. Initiate clings the globe that the educators are no more the single imparters of understanding; however, they require encouraging the pupils to find out at speed and their recreation via individual knowing networks maintaining their unique attributes of skills and the rate of interests. The instructors do not wind up after the course mores than yet on the shock for 24-hour around the cyber affiliation or social media networks even more. There is no wall surface currently or the limit of discovery. The cutting-edge instructor needs to develop an individual understanding network for their enhancement initially. Not just this, it needs to reach the pupils too, wherein there is no border of restriction in an effective means. It is a method to develop ones' very own class as well as one's very own network of knowing. The adjustment or the change right here is that we can share suggestions that are not so in the one to numerous settings of class discovering.

The connection through the cloud neighborhood is terrific and to the reach of bulk. It appears amusing to some, yet the reality continues to betray us that the highly Indian Education and learning System is just one of the unique educational program aspects in the nation at the same level as the establishing ones. It is excellent and among the prospering with the march of establishing a society of WWW (Whatever, When Ever Before as well as Wherever) pressure of finding out stage by the masses. Our students today are SMART, viz. Methodical, Careful, Imaginative, Reasonable, and Skillful in obtaining the best type of education and learning. We are making use of the abilities of exceptional databases and a society of Understanding by doing. No question, the application of ICT-based findings will provide a fillip to the needed experience effectively. The restrictions show up randomly but mirror the vibrant suggestions and possibilities using financial investments in the order of facilities, understanding centers, and mentor abilities. We eagerly anticipate an understanding center in the nation providing rates to the international Colleges quickly. What is required is an expertise culture incorporated with a guild of learners and lectures at a typical wavelength of understanding and supplying the knowledge.

The educators have a new notion now to be learners of age with the new vocabulary of A for Android, B for Blackberry, and C for Cloud. Counts for concern and a change mindset!!

CHAPTER NINE

School Leaders' Lessons on Pandemic

Taking control of the scenario, we need to build up our emotions and thoughts to stay

positive. This has to be the key to dealing with the anxiety amid the COVID-19 pandemic. The priority goes with the inception of protection of our personal space and staying away from the negative news as the new normal.

Friends, we all are affected by the pandemic and it has had a devastating impact on our community. The business is being shut, the schools, colleges and offices are being shut owning to the lockdown. The induced lockdown impacted the economy as several businesses were hit. For sure, the educators have come out to rescue via the Social Emotional Learning and Teaching to the students and the community at large as parents.

The teachers are constantly looking for better ways to motivate, engage and teach students whether the students are in class or at home. If not act well and respond to the alarming loss for our children, the loss of our children will literally prove to be a loss of 3 years in a row. We hereby introduce the challenges, best practices, available tools and resources to overcome the impact of covid-19 on the education sector.

The enriching contributions by some of the education leaders relate to the learning and a take away from the pandemic a new model to the new normal in particular.

Guest Writer

STAYING MOTIVATED DURING CHALLENGING TIMES

In a discussion over the pandemic, an optimist remarked "Well, hold on, this too will pass." And there reacted the pessimist "But when and how? There is no ray of hope." The optimist asserted "there is light at the end of the tunnel." Replied the pessimist "But how would you walk through this tunnel in this darkness? It is absolutely unsafe." The argument between the optimist and the pessimist is eternal over such issues in the pages of history and philosophy. And such dialogues are relevant to Covid too! Many asked the question "How did Covid enter this country? How did we allow it to come? Why did not we take precautions?" Questions relating to a post-mortem of events are a pastime for those who are unwilling to engage with meaningful action. Says Leon Trotsky – "You may not be interested in the war, but the war is interested in you". How true it is for Covid!

Though the onslaught of Covid has been seriously impacting many lives the world over, the fear, the panic, the mistrust, the suspicion created alongside had its toll on the human psyche. Many people lost their inner strength, their enthusiasm, their sense of enterprise and started sensing gloom. It reminds me of the famous saying of Leon Trotsky "You may not be interested in the war, but the war is interested in you" As true warriors, we need to rise up and stay motivated and nobody can motivate us unless we chose to do it for ourselves. Says Robin Sharma, noted author and speaker "No one can defeat you unless you are defeating yourself". How do we motivate ourselves? It is important to understand that each one of us has great latent power within us and we have to unlock the potential within.

You have a passion for writing poetry or a story. Please go ahead, you don't have to get it celebrated in a magazine, but the very fact that you have unleashed your power of fantasy and imagination will give you a sense of achievement and happiness.

You are interested in music. Enjoy your tunes and rhythm, not because you are going to be branded a superhero on a screen, but you declare yourself as a superhero of your own life, every song of yours will be the message of your soul and you will find how rich you are!

You have a reading habit. You won't find a better time to hug your books and plunge into their depth to discover the treasure of centuries of wisdom. You will not only acquire but conquer friends seen and unseen from ages, who will not only talk to you but counsel you to uplift your morale.

You are a techno-maniac. Hey! It is time to unravel the world of knowledge and skills through the portals of your computers. You will wander through many parts of the globe just from your own place and at no cost! Upgrade your understanding of this universe and the people.

In all these exercises and in several others, you attempt to bridge your "Being with Becoming". It will be a fabulous experience. We are blessed with a time for reflection, re-engineering and redefining our life. Get-Set and Go! Never succumb to fear and gloom! Says R.W. Emerson "The creation of a thousand forests is in one acorn" That is the power of a human being. He adds "What lies behind you and what lies in front of you, pales in comparison to what lies inside of you". It is time to unravel the treasure within!

G. Balasubramanian, Former Director (Academics), CBSE, New Delhi

Keeping Yourself Motivated during the current scenario!

Motivation is an intrinsic drive to, which enables you to break the cliché and move ahead with a positive affirmation. The unprecedented times brought the world to a steering halt, everything seemed topsy turvy and a whirlpool of negative emotions started pushing individuals to an echo chamber of uncertainty, anxiety and fear. I believe in the power of the mind, in fact, it all begins from the mind, as you think; so, shall be. While the outer world slowed down the inner world started an empathetic journey with a grateful heart. Collaboration, handholding and learning from one another became the new norm, people from across the globe started collaborating and sharing their expertise with one another. While the world was fighting with covid, the webinars kept people busy taking them to new learning landscapes. While there was enough stimulation for the mind to learn, keeping and staying fit became the need of the hour, healthy mind, healthy body, positive thoughts and giving back to society, helping the ones who are less privileged became the norm to fight back and to overcome the prevailing situation. A growth mindset helped me set my sails during the worst times and my journey from unlearning, relearn and learning kept pushing me to the new terrains of life.

I firmly believe that every situation has a solution, there is a light at the end of the tunnel all we need to do it, to hold on to hope and be true to ourselves and our work.

Be like a river and keep on making your way, keep on flowing keep on moving ahead breaking all barriers...and while moving, forward is the only direction.

Further, the person in the mirror, motivated me, inspired me, questioned me and led me to do more, to be more & to achieve more, because woods are lovely dark and deep, but I have promises to keep and miles to go before I sleep...& miles to go before I sleep.

As an educator, the disaster driven digitalisation, not only changed the learning landscapes for me but gave me an opportunity to step into the parent's shoes, while they stepped into educators. We are riding on the tide of a culture of constant change and this process made the educators like me become lighthouses; lighthouses to guide everyone equally without any biases and illuminate each and every life they come across.

Last, but not least, feed your mind with positivity and wisdom. Discipline is a must in life and giving priority to yourself needs to be at the top of every day's to-do list. I follow a simple routine I practice gratitude and empathy, which keeps me mentally and emotionally calm and one hour of physical exercise, 5 days a week is a ritual for me. Also, when you make the mirror your biggest critic, you very well know what do you want to see. So, be the best version of yourself; mentally and physically, emotionally and lookup for opportunities amidst the adversities; all we need to do is change our lenses to see that life is beautiful and we need to live it to the fullest, every day.

Dr. Seema Negi, Global Goodwill Ambassador, Life Coach, Director Principal, Sanjeevani World School, Mumbai, India.

Beating Covid my way.

When I reflect upon the year gone by, I look at it as a year of great learning. I have always believed that learning never ends because life never stops teaching us. This Covid time has reinforced that and taught me resilience, collaboration, communication and critical thinking. It has helped me push my limits and discover more. Most importantly, it gave me an insight into various nuances of life and the time to reflect and look inwards.

Education has evolved and given wings of opportunities to today's learners. The seamless transition of my school to the online mode is a proof of that. The rigours were felt and dealt with, and the transformation into online classes, activities, interactions, learning tools, resources, massive open online free courses and apps came to the rescue of students. Today there is no dearth of possibilities, even when the student body remains confined to their homes. Indeed, we our spirit has been tested but we emerged victorious.

My institution and I have worked in tandem and our desire to give the students a wholesome education has blessed all of us with positivity and hope. We grow each day, replicating all school activities online with the same spirit and value as the offline ones. Online classes have been enriched with ICT tools and suggested hands-on activities. School competitions and co-curricular activities like debates, talent fests, MUNs, Sports Day, Class wise presentations and orientations were successfully conducted. Other important developmental monitoring segments such as Career counseling sessions, Parent-Teacher meetings, Interaction of students with professional experts were also organized. And are still marching on, undeterred.

Keeping in mind that the continuous lockdowns will deter students from availing texts, practice workbooks and papers we have also worked on our very own MOODLE, which is a robust learning platform or course management system (CMS). It is a software package designed to help educators create effective online resources for students .

My love and passion to remain in touch with my students, inspired me to create a free learning App, iBrainPower which has research-proven strategies that can effectively improve memory, enhance recall, and increase retention of information. I also launched a course about 'training the brain' on Udemy, a MOOC.

Parent-community also needed special attention hence I started a series of talks on YouTube called 'Parent to Parent-Man Ki Baat' to motivate the parents to develop the resilience to cope with whatever life throws at them and become socially and emotionally strong.

These unprecedented times have taught me like never before and owing to my determination, I was able to record, edit, compile and upload all my digital content singlehandedly. The world is battling with new challenges, unlearning and relearning. To keep at it is the key to growth. My firm belief in the power of learning especially in a storm like Covid, is reiterated in the words of Louisa May Alcott , " I am not afraid of storms for I am learning how to sail my ship."

Dr Anshu Arora, CBSE awardee & Principal of Amity International School, Gurugram has over 27 years of teaching & administrative experience. She co-authored the CBSE Handbook for students & NCC Manual. She has authored fictions, non-fictions and poetry books. She is an administrator, educator, author, speaker & a lifelong 'Learner'.

5 most beneficial ways to keep yourself motivated during these difficult times

The COVID-19 pandemic has shaken our lives and the world in a multitude of ways. After months of being stuck at home has given birth to several problems. Limited exposure to friends and family members and most importantly juggling between home and office responsibilities have resulted in anger, low morale, frustration, and much more. Some of the studies have shown that a positive outlook and mindset can help balance both mind and body. Being positive is to face challenges with great will power and help each other during these unprecedented times.

It is quite possible that most of you find it arduous to keep yourself motivated. But worry not, we are here with the most beneficial ways to keep you positive:

Make a routine- Kick start your day by waking up early and workout to stay positive and energized. Make a to-do list with all the tasks related to work and personal chores you want to accomplish during the day. The to- do list will help you to keep a track of what needs to be done and help you be prepared for the next day.

Paint, sing or read a book- We all have certain hobbies and this is the best time that we must begin spending more time doing our favourite things. This will give you ample happiness and be quite healing as well. So, why wait? Take out those paintbrushes or a book to get engrossed in your favourite stuff.

Stay calm and relax- There is so much going on outside that it is vital for you to get offline from all this and breathe. It is not always important to listen and watch everything on social media and television. Filter out things and spend your valuable time listening to good songs, watching movies, cooking, and much more. Take out time to appreciate nature and take a walk in your garden and spend some quality time with your family.

Schedule virtual get-togethers- Yes, your friends and family members are the most important people in your life. Meeting them is not possible these days but you can talk to them through video calls and feel great. Plan out the time and make the best use of the same to play games and chit-chat. These little joys will definitely make you happy and motivated.

Prioritize your mental health- Staying positive during these times can be a bit difficult. But, if we continue doing this, it can turn to be negative for our mental health. Exercise, talk to your friends and family, read books and have a good diet. Taking care of yourself is the foremost thing. Stay positive to beat the odds as you can do it.

It is not too late, prep up yourself and create a beautiful and cheerful world for yourself. There is no benefit in sitting and worrying about things as it will only take a toll on your mental health. Do not forget that you have come this far. You are stronger than you think!

Remember, this too shall pass!

Dr. Sangeeta, PhD. in Design & Architecture with hands on experience of 22+ years; she is a Founder & Principal Interior Designer of Urban Interiors, a brand for top-notch residential and bespoke commercial projects. She is the Global Ambassador of Design & Architecture 2021, a National Awardee with "Life Real Hero Achiever's Award 2019" and "The Resolute Achiever's Global Women's Award 2020". Being the Chairperson of MENTORx Women and a renowned woman empowerer, she has is working towards educating, empowering, and elevating women from all walks of life. She is also the Assistant Vice President of MSMECCII and Editor in Chief - Haryana, Police Suraksha Magazine, Regd. by Ministry of I & B, Govt. of India. She is a Mentor and a Global Influencer.

The Most deadly Pandemic *after the Bubonic Plague that hit Humanity in 1920 is the Covid -19 virus that has spread globally and completely turned our world upside down as we knew it before 2020 . Everything looks so surreal isn't it ? Corona- virus has impacted people in various ways on an international level with a feeling of fear, concern and anxiousness with all the uncertainty and constantly changing alerts with regards to the spread of the virus.*

In such a unprecedented situation each one of us is left with just two choices either to face this Pandemic with Optimism or to face it with Pessimism. I agree it's not easy to be Optimistic in the said situation but it is a collective challenge which we all need to face by keeping a positive mindset during these turbulent times being faced by humanity in search of that silver lining.

We must attempt to enter a state of acceptance and use our energy positively to build stronger, physical & mental health of our community regardless of the isolation we face whilst tackling this virus. It's been over 14 months of uncertainity and of course, these limitations on our freedom are definitely taxing because human beings aren't meant to live in isolation like this.

Personally, I chose the optimistic route and I'd like to share with you some ways on how to remain positive during this time in order to make this challenging period a little lighter mentally and emotionally, resulting in inevitable benefits.

Set aside time for daily Prayers & Meditation

Spend time with your family cooking, gardening, playing board games etc.

Set short-term goals that aren't taxing, but will keep you motivated.

Limit your exposure to Media & News Channels as this can increase feelings of fear and anxiety.

Create a routine that priorities things you like doing and even things you have been wanting to do but haven't had enough time for.

Connect with family and friends virtually.

Enroll in Online Courses.

Indulge in Social Service Activities.

Stay Physically Active.

Practice Yoga, Deep Breathing, Walk, Exercise or Play your favourite game.

Eating nutritious and immunity boosting food and keep yourself hydrated.

Seek Emotional & Expert Psychological support if needed.

Watch movies with your family to have a positive mindset and practice random acts of kindness.

As hard as the current situation we are in and as hopeless the situation may seem, there is light at the end of the tunnel...

Have faith in God & Hold on strong and I assure you before long we will all reconnect physically back into our beautiful world.

*Tina Olyai is a founder director of Little Angels School in Gwalior, in her journey of 31 years as Director of LAHS Gwalior the school has effectively served it's mission to mould thousands of children into intellectual & virtuous human beings. Our Alumni are radiating their glory in every corner of the globe, proving their excellence in myriad fields of human endeavours. She quotes: "Recognitions smell sweet ! I am truly grateful to God that I have been acclaimed for various contributions in the field of education on a number of occasions. " *Recipient of `Most Popular Personality Amongst Educational Heads' *Awarded `Lady of the Month` by Dainik Bhaskar Group. *Selected amongst 'The Top 15 Achievers of the State of Madhya Pradesh' by The Times of India. *Featured in Times of India Coffee Table Book TRAILBLAZERS.*

*Awarded on International Women's Day as an 'Outstanding Educationist of Gwalior'. *Zee TV recognised me as one of the 'Top 15 Powered Persons of Madhya Pradesh'. *Zee TV also featured me in its Coffee Table Book as among "Top 15 Powerful Figures of Madhya Pradesh & Chhattisgarh", *The Chief Minister of Madhya Pradesh Shri Shivraj Singh Chouhan, conferred on me the Honour of being amongst the 'Top 20 Leading Business Visionaries of 2010'. *Awarded by Shrimant Yashodhara Raje Scindia, Minister of Commerce, Industries and Employment, Madhya Pradesh on Womens Day. *Recieved the SEAS Global Women Achiever Award, *Selected by Education today as Leaders the Pillars in Education. *Recognized as Top 50 Visionaries by Education India.*

KEEPING YOURSELF MOTIVATED DURING THIS PANDEMIC

A pessimist sees a problem in every opportunity, and an optimist sees an opportunity in every problem.

No one is exempted from trials and tribulations of life yet it is up to us how we look at things and situations. Life has never been fair .Poetic justice never seems to reign in real life. In fact, it is a far fetched notion that seems to prevail only in fiction . So how can we change our situations whilst we have no control over them. Can't we remould the way we think and the way we perceive things. There is a way out of falling into the ditch of depression from where a come back may be challenging. We can always try to find something positive even in the worst of situations. Is it that difficult?

• 57 •

The Covid Pandemic is one of its kind. It has disrupted, in fact corroded our smooth going lives . With the clampdown on movements ,be it due to a series of lockdowns or sensible self-imposed or forced quarantine, many of us are stuck within the four walls of our home, unable to visit our family and friends. The "work from home" formula seems you have traded our "travelling time" with our 'personal time'. Many of us have lost our jobs and regular source of income, schools have been temporarily shut down leaving parents even more perplexed with not only household chores but also co-educating their kids with teachers. All this has led to a conglomeration of never ever experienced emotions. Even those who claim to be level headed and emotionally strong have succumbed to the unexpected and unwelcomed whirlpool of poignant situations. Therefore, it comes as no surprise that thousands and millions of us are wrestling with negative thoughts, grappling with loneliness and dealing with constant sense of despair and frustration. If you think you are the only one, who is not able to handle the ongoing situation and living in an environment where there seems to be no ray of hope, then you are mistaken.

But wait. There is an option. You always had one. Either, you can collapse under the pressure of this pandemic and give up whatever hope you have got or, gather that fistful of hope , fight like a warrior and rise like the phoenix.

Let us promise to be a fighter and remember how optimism can tilt the odds in the your favour. Let me share a few strategies which will surely help you keep motivated and away from negativity and hopelessness.

Accept the situation and strategize Acknowledging one's situation is the foremost step to get out of a negative environment. Gather all your mental and emotional strength and chart out a way to come out of it. Don't hesitate to take help from your near and dear ones.

Invest in self-care: The age old saying a healthy mind lives in a healthy body still stands relevant. Get up, take a walk on your terrace or in your balcony or within your room, stretch your body, engage yourself in yoga and do light exercises. Inhale positivity and hope with enough oxygen in your lungs and exhale all negative thoughts and keep a smile on your face.

Engage yourself in your favourite activity and Stay Productive When we engage ourselves in our favourite work, we feel relaxed and our mind becomes stable and a sense of achievement sets in. You can read a book, take care of plants, play with your children, solve Sudoku, decorate your room, groom yourself.... the list is endless.

Talk, express and share your thoughts: Don't stay silent and live in your imaginary world. Rather speak out . It will help to vent out your emotions.

Filter your source of information: News channel are flooded with fake and distressful information. Do watch the news channel but take in only the relevant information and don't allow any negative information disturb your state of mind.

Try to learn a skill: Learn a new skill from your parent, your sibling or from internet. Learning a new skill will always help in bringing a sense of achievement and groom you into a better person.

Design a Schedule :A Schedule would help you in organising your task and keep you active throughout the day. It would give you enough time to reflect upon your situation.

Make Gratitude your Attitude: Feel blessed to have a life which many others might have been deprived of. Remember, one should never take everything for granted . Cherish and celebrate the small joys of life.

This unprecedented pandemic has compelled every one of us to alter our behaviour, whether we like it not. The ongoing situation feels endless but believe me, everything has an end and this will end too one day. Above all remember, Worrying doesn't empty tomorrow of its sorrows but it empties today of its strengths. So, Keep smiling and stay motivated.

Ms. Alka Kapur, (CBSE and State Awardee), Principal, Modern Public School, Shalimar Bagh, Delhi is an empowering leader, a zealous educationist with rich academic and administrative experience offering an illustrious career as a principal spanning 21 years in educational research. As the Principal of the school, she has taken the school to great heights through open attitude for learning and love for children. Twenty one years of her sedulous selfless service has accorded the school a priceless status in Forbes India Marquee Edition, The Great Indian Schools. She is a recipient of more than 50 accolades at National, International and State level including CBSE Teachers' and Principals' Award 2019-2020 by Shri. Ramesh Pokhriyal 'Nishank' Hon'ble Minister of Education, Mahatma Gandhi Samman Award at House of Lords, London, Progressive Principal of India award, Humanity excellence award, Educational reformer of the year,

Best Principal award from the Ambassador of Latvia, Ambassador vision knowledge by Indian Federation of United Nations association and many more. At present, Ms Alka Kapur is the President, Delhi Sahodaya School Complex, Vice-President Indraprastha School Sahodaya, Member of National Progressive School Conference, Action Committee unaided recognised Public Schools and Forum of Public Schools. She holds the position of State Convener, New Delhi, Global Edu – Leader Forum and is a member of FICCI ARISE COMMITTEE. She encompasses her vision of making the world beautiful by spreading the light of education through her pious efforts, meticulous work, infinite patience endowed with divine blessings.

Keeping yourself motivated even during the current scenario

You may feel as if your life has suddenly flipped upside down and your motivation is at an all-time low because we are all using social distancing strategies and the majority of us are home-based. You're not alone, after all!

This, like every other difficult period in history, will pass, and we will emerge stronger. Meanwhile, it's vital to remember that even if you're stuck at home, there are methods to keep your mind balanced and motivated.

1. Set simple daily objectives.

It's critical to remember that these aren't regular times, and your performance isn't going to be at its best right now. And that's fine. Setting daily objectives can help you make the most of your day, but be practical with your expectations. Make sure they're not too high or you'll be disappointed in yourself.

2. Make a schedule that includes both work and leisure.

Working from home might make it difficult to resist the desire to work continuously or to become easily distracted by television or other household items... leading to the sensation that you are not achieving the tasks you set for yourself. You may achieve a healthy work-life balance at home by scheduling when you will work and when you will rest.

3. Make virtual get-togethers with pals a priority.

The worst element of this epidemic might be social separation, especially for folks who appreciate the social side of coming together.

But you don't have to stop doing so, and you don't have to give up your social life.

4. Make your mental health a top priority.

It is critical that you manage your stress and concerns at this time. If you're having trouble staying motivated, take a look at your hurdles. Make sure you get some exercise every day, even if it's simply a walk around your block or neighbourhood, to keep your mental health in check.

5. Accept the fact that you won't be very productive right now.

You may discover that some days you are really driven and do more things than you intended, while other days you are completely unfocused. It's ok; nothing is normal at the moment, and we all need to pay attention to ourselves. Go over your to-do list and prioritise what needs to be done today against what can wait until tomorrow.

A couple additional suggestions

Let go of whatever shame you may have felt for not being successful. Take each day as an opportunity to start over. Look for bright moments wherever you can find them, such as strangers helping strangers, teachers checking in on students, and communities banding together. Consider putting some restrictions on how much you watch the news or read about the covid-19. If you need help, reach out to those who you trust.

Dr. Malka Grewal is a Principal at Britannica International school, Ludhiana (Cambridge affiliated), a CAIE Exam Officer, Director, Kids Captivation (A chain of Play Schools), Resource Trainer for English Linguistics, TEFL Trainer (Cambridge), Cambridge English- Train the Trainer, Proficiency Scaffolder in global contexts, Recipient of various International & National Awards.

Self Motivation is the key to unlock the potential within you.
Make things happen !!! Do not give up !!!!

Do what you love. Take some time out and talk to yourself. Self talk helps a lot. Be careful with you word when you talk to urself. Use positive and inspiring words. Keep appreciating yourself for your good work.

Manage your expectations. Keep small achievable goals.

Surround yourself with people who are positive

in their thoughts and words and motivate you. They will help you Reframe, Redirect and Refocus your goals when it gets tough.

No matter how small your achievement is, celebrate your success.

Paint beautiful vision of your future.Be so self motivated yourself that you are an inspiration for others

Best part of this pandemic scenario is the extent to which digitalisation has shrunk the world. Thanks to Zoom, MEET, Teams, getting connected with global counterparts has become very easy. Plan online get togethers and celebrations.

Information is good but limit yourself to reading pandemic-related news for only a short amount of time but not in the morning. Stay informed from reputable sources, but avoid getting wrapped up in constant news coverage that will only heighten anxiety. Allow yourself time to enjoy TV and social media, but try to reduce how much time you spend listening to pandemic news.

Taking care of yourself can help you to better manage your mental health during this time. Maintain a normal sleep schedule, and aim to get at least eight hours of sleep a night. Hv a healthy balanced diet and exercise regularly.

Some days you may not have much ability to focus at all, and that's to be expected! Nobody's life is normal right now. You may find that you have good days where you're highly motivated to get through work and bad days where your motivation is nowhere to be found. It's okay to expect less from yourself right now.

Lockdown!!!! Yes everyone is locked up !!! But this is the best time to unlock ur potential!!! You might be working from home still try to maintain the similar routine. Get dressed the way you wud if u had to travel to work.

Don't lose focus of your goals. Force yourself to keep going forward. This too shall pass !!!

Dr. Ushavati Shetty, Principal, Navodaya English High School & Jr. College, Thane, Maharashtra- India

KEEPING YOURSELF MOTIVATED EVEN DURING THE CURRENT SCENARIO

2020....The world almost came to a standstill due to the pandemic. The disruption we are facing is unlike anything we have faced before. It is legitimate for us to feel frustration, anger and more as a result of the multitude of ways in which our lives have changed. How do we stay motivated right now, more than one year into a pandemic with no end in sight?

CHANGE AND MODIFY YOUR EXPECTATIONS Now is not the time, I would say, to pretend these are normal times. Acknowledging and accepting that it is OK to not feel inspired as we did in 2019 is the first step to help us adjust to this new normal. Everyone is struggling right now and the world is going through collective grief. Telling yourself 'I am not alone in this and it is perfectly okay to not be highly productive now ' is the first step to have collective motivation to sail through unprecedented times.

STAY CONNECTED Loneliness, isolation and challenges to mental health have been major by-products of the pandemic and these are impacting our resilience in these difficult times. Having a support network of friends, family and peer can help people get through these periods of trauma and improve their ability to respond to stress, Remaining connected even at a distance during even the strictest of lockdowns is so salutary. Have you ever surprised yourself, when walking around, adopting all sanitary norms, by " Oh! I am alive! There are people around me!"? Everything is not doom and gloom. This is motivation to carry on.

TRANSFORM CHALLENGES INTO OPPORTUNITIES A matchless gift given to us by the pandemic is undoubtedly time which can be used to transform challenges into opportunities to innovate, succeed and grow both individually and professionally. The education sector is one of the most impacted ones in current times. Many education stakeholders have remained motivated even globally by connecting through digital platforms during webinars, webifairs and by sharing resources. Building up soft skills during this period through virtual internships and other activities has been a great source of motivation for students. On a personal note, my most amazing experience has been having my students from Mauritius participating enthusiastically in a virtual MUN Conference hosted by Sri Ram College of Commerce, Delhi University! Create opportunities for yourself with what is globally available.

INVEST IN SELF-CARE Navigating this new normal is not easy, creating a need to motivate ourselves to take care of our own health- all aspects of it by investing in simple things that make a huge difference in our mental state.

Prioritising good-quality sleep to keep our immune system running properly

Exercising and adopting healthy eating habits

Doing a creative hobby

Reading (something inspiring definitely helps)

Listening to music

Trying something altogether new to you and above all

Maintaining happiness for yourself and your environment.

We are living in a time that is unusually challenging but we have a choice – either to succumb to the pressure and give up or stay motivated to not only get through but come out even better than before.

WHEN ALL IS WELL, WE ARE GOING TO LOOK BACK ON THIS PERIOD OF OUR LIVES AND BE GLAD WE NEVER GAVE UP.

Prabha Doonanath, Lecturer, Mauritius. A student-focused dedicated educator, Prabha DHOONOOAH is currently working as Chemistry teacher, Dean of Studies and School Counselor at College du Saint Esprit, Mauritius. She has 30+ years of experience in the field of education.

'Every cloud has a silver lining'.....and we should follow this during this pandemic situation.

Covid-19 of course is causing havoc but we should never lose hope. If we think positive everything becomes positive and if we keep on thinking about negative things it does turn into negative. We should keep ourselves busy in different types of job, it may be household job, it may be our hobbies, it may be our passion for gardening, reading books etc. We should make a timetable ready for us, our daily routine which we used to follow before will now slightly change. Previously we often heard people saying that due to my busy schedule I hardly have time to even speak to my relatives or even give quality time to my family....but now we can. Covid-19 has taught us certain things, earlier we became too busy with our work, we started maintaining gratuitous associations, but now we are very cautious about hygiene; we hardly go out and meet people physically. We don't mind being house arrested just to save our family members.

We can self motivate ourselves:

1. We can set daily targets: It helps us a lot, as end of the day you feel good as you did not waste your day. You could achieve what wanted. It may be very simple thing like arranging your wardrobe, completing 5 pages of your story book, learning a dish etc.

2. Being socially active: You may meet your friends and relatives through digital meeting platforms and keep in touch with each other or to pursue all official jobs. This way you don't feel lonely and you share your feelings with others.

3. Take care of your mental and physical health: You are responsible for your happiness and sadness. Nobody can make you happy or sad. It is your responsibility to keep yourself fit and fine. You should go for exercise every day, eat healthy, drink plenty of water and limit yourself to reading pandemic related news and avoid getting wrapped up in constant news coverage that will only increase your anxiety.

4. Give time to yourself: Whatever makes you happy, Just do it! It may be cooking, watching movies, stitching, playing video games, gardening, painting, gossiping(virtually) anything that makes you feel happy. Go ahead and keep yourself charged.

5. Extending help to others: At this difficult point of time it is essential to extend helping hands to others in various ways. Many social activists or NGOs selflessly working day and night to serve the society by offering food, oxygen, medicines, ambulance service to name a few. By helping others at their difficult time one can achieve immense happiness. But yes, while extending helps to others no one should forget to take the necessary self protection measures.

Last but not the least ,though it's my personal feeling if anybody requires any sort of help we may extend it to them ,sometimes even some motivating words makes a huge difference.

TIME AND TIDE WAITS FORNONE, NOTHING IS STATIC IN THIS WORLD....SO STAY POSITIVE, HELP OTERS, STAY SAFE AND TAKE CARE.

Dr. Nandita Nandi, Principal, TECHNO INDIA GROUP PUBLIC SCHOOL, Siliguri Campus, West Bengal. Dr. Nandita Nandi is associated in this education field for last 21 years. A recipient of many awards and recognitions from reputed Universities or institutions. She has 15 research publications in different peer reviewed International and National journals. She has presented her research papers on Child Psychology in various coveted conferences.

Learning during Covid

Amidst this global crisis of the pandemic that mankind is facing from the past one year, the face of normalcy has changed. It has also reformed the way our education system functioned. The transformation in the educational landscape, ability to provide the support to students, upskilling the teachers, collaborating with parents; almost everything in educational institutes faced the tectonic shift.

In the middle of countless challenges, one does not have a second choice except to remain motivated to ensure that the ship continues moving especially when you are in a position to lead the team irrespective you are losing family, friends or loved ones. It reminded me of a quote from one of my favourite books, "Man's search for meaning" by Victor Frankl. It states that one who has the why to live can endure almost any 'How.'

Fortunately, I could identify that 'WHY' quickly. The safety & wellbeing of children besides ensuring their learning; at-least those in my radar, was the reason larger than anything else in this world. God has been kind to me all through my personal and professional life but this time, the objective of my life became clearer than ever.

The first task was to train teachers to equip them with technology for supporting students, be online, offline, blended or hybrid learning. For using platforms from Zoom to G-Meet and Teams, contacting parents through WhatsApp to direct call, using padlet, storyboard to mentimeter for engaging students while teaching, G-form to kahoot for assessment; teachers were trained during virtual meetings almost every alternate day. Hats off to the families of teachers for their untiring and unconditional support. Personally, I will always be indebted to them.

The next challenging task was to convince parents about online classes. Withstanding strong against the negative media influence, teachers contacted parents individually. The team of teachers faced disappointments but everyone had infinite belief in herself which got synergised. The faith of parents was recouped. Exemptions or financial relaxation were given. Classes were provided at differential timing considering the availability of mobile phones at a home where siblings were attending the classes. The teachers ensure to keep the parents engaged and motivated during this tough time through different events and competitions for parents and grand-parents. It really worked well. Sharing our schedule and plan with parents during virtual PTM and inspiring them with a bigger dream for their children booted the learning further.

The keywords to conclude my learning during pandemic are teamwork, collaboration, strong value system and service before self. 'The time is always right to do what is right,' said Martin Luther King, Jr. There is enough for everyone on this earth provided we receive our pile and share it with a smile.

The world is in a odd state but everything will still turn worse unless each one of us do our best selflessly. The passionate educators are amongst those worriers whose tenacious endeavour is to design the path towards educating children with the right attitude besides skills and knowledge. At American International School, the team of teachers is inclined to do their best bit with the firm faith that this time of crises will pass and children will spread the essence of their learning when they bloom. My team along with me ensured that although the gates of the temples of learning are closed, the learning should always continue.

Jai Hind.

Dr Mukta Misra, Director, American International School, Greater Noida. Associated with school education from the past 37 years., Completed research in Strategic Leadership in School Education, Did Masters in subjects English, Economics, Education., Made presentations at national and International conferences, Conducted more than numerous workshops for school teachers, Resource Person of CBSE and also a British

Council School Ambassador, Authored 45 books so far, Published articles in educational magazines, Work acknowledged by various NGOs, CBSE and Directorate of Education, Govt. of NCT Delhi.

"Magic Mantra for Motivation"

Our mind is nothing short of a miracle, if you understand its working and its power. It has the capacity to heal as well as the ability to make you fall sick. If you believe that your mind is the CEO of your body and your life, you will begin to pay more heed to it and awaken its potential. As a species, we are the most advanced neurologically and hence superior, but psychologically and spiritually we are failing miserably and hence suffer. At most times, our mind is split as our thoughts, attitudes, emotions and actions are not integrated.

It would be important to understand a few philosophical truths about the pandemic. One fact is that all of us as a human race, globally, are in a mode of 'survival' and not 'thriving'. Hence these are abnormal and ambiguous times. The second truth is that we can do nothing about it but 'accept it gracefully' and allow the time to pass. The third truth is that it's a time for 'adaptation and adjustment' to the new mode of life. The huge dinosaur with a weight of 70 tonnes became extinct due to its inability to adapt and the cockroach continues to survive due to its ability to adapt! Taking inspiration from a cockroach let's do what we are expected to do in the circumstances and not what we would like to do. 'What does the current circumstances expect me to do' is the question you should address yourself? The answers will lead you on.

Many things might de-motivate you as we all know the restrictions the lockdown has imposed on us. You are not alone. Motivation is a continuous process of keeping yourself energised with good thoughts, positive emotions, a sense of gratitude for all the blessings in your life, and engaging in creative and happy activities and goals. Take the current situation as a challenge and as an opportunity to grow and expand your talents and skills. This is the best time to invest in yourself. Motivation is more intrinsic than extrinsic and depends a lot on inner controls. A person with a strong mind likes to be in control of the situation rather than become a victim.

Besides your aspirations and goals which might seem to be thwarted at the moment, you also have a 'duty', a 'dharm', to perform. Those who understand the nature of their 'dharm', keep engaged in doing it dispassionately. Duty is performed with a sense of discipline and equanimity. You might be a student, teacher, administrator, doctor, nurse or homemaker, your sense of duty will keep you engaged in your work. A good singer, dancer or artist practices minimum eight hours a day with a sense of dedication, with no positive or negative emotion. Take charge of your mind, maintain a sense of calmness, and keep doing what you are supposed to do as your duty with discipline! That is the magic mantra!

Rita Aggarwal. Consultant Psychologist, Nagpur. A Gold medallist in Psychology at her Masters and Bachelors, Rita brings 35 years of accomplished experience in the field of psychology, and has established herself as the leading Pioneer of psychological counselling in Central India since she went independent in 1990 in Nagpur. Her skills and contribution have been recognised by her nomination as the Chapter Champion for the TIE Global project for women entrepreneurs named AIRSWEE 1.0 and All India Director for AIRSWEEE 2.0 and 3.0, funded by the State Department of United States of America.

'The difference between stumbling blocks and stepping stones is how you use them,'. *This quote by Benny Lewis perfectly describes our current situation and how we must survive it with a positive spirit. The pandemic caused by Covid-19, led to a home quarantine situation for most of us and brought with itself several unpleasant situations and swarmed our minds with pessimistic thoughts and feelings. In the* midst of this once in a lifetime battle unfolding, we have forgotten about all the good in life. With our health (mental and physical) which is at its very low, staying. motivated and looking at the bright side has become a very difficult task. Living within the same walls of our homes for the past year and more, stress of working from home, fear of getting infected by this deadly virus, surviving this deadly virus, not being able to meet loved ones, and many more such instances have led to us being pessimistic all the time.

Personally, for me, this period, has been a roller coaster ride of joyous as well as saddened feelings. On one side there has been the much-desired space and time to bond with my family and on the other side there have been situations where I felt I would break down and all I wanted to do was give up, but I could not for the sake of my own mental and physical health, my family, work and other causes. The loop of negative thinking and actions led me to push myself to get out of it and made me realize the power of motivation (self and external) and its importance in keeping you going.

When the pandemic started unfolding and the idea of home quarantine came into being, everyone including me was very confused. It was new territory, something none of us had *ever experienced. To stay at one place all year without leaving the threshold of the house, seemed comical two years ago. Now it is our reality, and honestly, it was baffling to come to terms with, to say the least. After an initial storming stage of living in this new reality, I started accepting it as a norm and decided to make the good out of all the free time I had by enhancing some of my skills. Rediscovering my long- lost interests added a new leash of life to my hobbies which was very refreshing and got me closer to my inner self.*

I realized the importance of family time together. Prior to the pandemic times, with my busy work schedules and my children's studies' schedules, we barely had time to sit and talk about our day. Being home bound for the entirety of a day made us come together and cherish each other. This was how we shaped our lives and built a positive frame that we operated around for a year since the pandemic had struck.

As the winter of this year started to say goodbye, I suddenly developed a stubborn fever and body aches. My secret fear came true when the report showed a positive – yes, I had been infected by the Corona virus.

Confined to a room, medications on, regular virtual check- ups, loss of taste and smell, a heavy head and a weak body- all of this took a heavy toll on me mentally and physically. Each news article I read made me doubt if I would make it to the next day and even a slight dip in the oximeter reading made me panic as if that was the end of my day. Fears for the welfare of my children and family started engulfing me and I found myself at the bottom of a well of physical and mental misery. It was at this time that my guardian angels came to my rescue and pushed me to save me from the perils of my monkey mind. I was lucky enough to have only mild symptoms and realised that indeed was a gift of life. I revived my Faith and Belief in the Almighty and let it absorb me in the teachings of life.

Just listening to the religious hymns from Guru Granth Sahab Ji, brought so much peace and serenity and made me forget about all the worries I had.

Reading the holy books, understanding their deeper meaning, made me realize there is so much more to life than we know and understand.

Faith and belief in God is what made me survive that difficult time and helped me tide over all my worries.

I also realized the importance of yoga and how it benefits our physical as well as mental health. It definitely was and still is one of my inspirations during this time.

I continue reshaping these times we face through life teachings I've had.

This pandemic and quarantine has made me realize the importance of faith and I believe that if we have faith and belief in anything- nature, God, science, or literally anything under the sun, and we trust what we believe in, we can survive this difficult time and we can come out as strong and better people after these trying times are over.

As I said on a starting note, till normal times are back, let's create stepping stones out of our stumbling blocks and motivate each other inspiring along the way.

Sharanjt Kaur is an educationist for last 15 years. Being the Principal of New Angel Public School, Chandigarh, she has made the holistic development of every child as her priority and is a proponet of the cause of education. In the current challenging times, she has kept the momentum going in terms of continued education and development and adapting the schooling infrastructure to the need of the hour. Described as a strict disciplinarian and a warm approachable leader at the same time, she takes on the current covid scenario, does show the way ahead through self motivation and faith.

KEEPING YOURSELF MOTIVATED EVEN DURING THE CURRENT SCENARIO

(From an Educator's perspective)

The world enters a second year living with the COVID-19 pandemic and half of the global student population is still affected by full or partial school closure. In this crisis, teachers have shown their great leadership and innovation in ensuring that 'Learning Never Stops' and 'No Learner is Left Behind'. Around the world, they have worked individually and collaboratively to find solutions and create new learning environments for their students to allow education to continue. They make a crucial contribution to ensuring continuity of learning and supporting the mental health and wellbeing of their students. A good quality education is the foundation of health and well-being. For people to lead healthy and productive lives, they need knowledge to prevent sickness and disease. Education is a catalyst for development and a health intervention in its own right. To build a more resilient teacher workforce in times of crisis, all teachers should be equipped with digital and pedagogical skills to teach remotely, online, and through blended or hybrid learning, whether in high-, low- or no-tech environments.

Everywhere, together with school leaders, teachers have been rapidly mobilizing and innovating to facilitate distance learning for students in confinement, with or without the use of digital technologies. They are playing a key role in communicating measures that prevent the spread of the virus and ensuring that children are safe and supported. Due to the closure of all educational institutions, students have been compelled to disrupt their daily routines. But this is a good time to instill compassion and kindness in the child. We can share heartwarming stories of young people, scientists, health workers, who are keeping the community safe.

We are living through a pandemic that most of us could never have imagined. During these challenging times, even caregivers such as teachers might end up feeling anxious or stressed. The job of a teacher extends far beyond education alone, however it's just as much about helping children build self-

confidence and a belief in them that will hopefully stay with them throughout the course of their adult lives. The time has come for all schools to address the missing link in what will help educators' thrive—a greater focus on all adults' health and well-being. It is important for teachers to first take care of themselves. Wellbeing is the combination of feeling good and functioning effectively. Taking the time to experience positive emotions can increase wellbeing during unpredictable times.

(From a counselor's perspective)

Every day is a unique day. No day comes off distinguishable. Be it the people that we attend, the knowledge gained, the distinctive stories that we listen to, or the challenges we encounter each day, they are all different from the ones before. When Covid-19 affected the lives of the whole

world in a way no one has anticipated, online counseling helped to reach out to a very large number of people who never had an access to counseling. Counselors could support their online clients with their emotional roller coaster.

Student counselors, Relationship Counselors, and most importantly Mental Health counselors had quite a large number of people reaching out to them during pandemic. Being on the verge of a health crisis, with an increasing number of deaths, isolation, and no socialization people who didn't have any history of mental illness found a happy survival difficult and started collapsing. Every counselor stepped into the lives of people that they have not met before and heard their poignant stories. With more and more people approaching counselors, the workload of counselors has taken up 3/4 of their day ending up giving them not enough time for themselves.

The mental state of a counselor has a tremendous impact on every session with a client and as such, self-care plays quite a significant role in a counselor's life. What we are and how we feel about ourselves have a direct impact on everyone who relies on us for support. In simple words, we can't share what we don't have. Counselors come across moment that makes them feel like it's a daunting race that has to be won. This is what makes the job of a counselor even more interesting as every counselor would have a hope that the race will end with a success where a one can witness changes in a client. These enduring changes paves way to motivation for every one of us who serves as a mental health professional.

The noticeable changes in every client serve as rewards that encourage, energize, and motivate every mental health professionals. Be it a school counselor getting in close contact with a child to help them with their medical and educational concerns, providing them with an intervention that can be employed at home, or a relationship counselor who is attending a client who would have never approached for support if it was an in-person session, every case attended gives a feeling of contentment and that acts a daily fair for every counselor.

Knowing that life is made better and easy for people who have approached counselors acts as a daily motivation or a daily dose of happiness. With enough self-care which is an essential part of mindfulness, and rewards received in the form of progress of clients, counseling will not be just any profession but a wisdom profession.

In these troubled times, it is essential for everyone to stay connected with friends and family virtually. The most important thing is finding the healthy habits that can make life easier, until

the things we can't control change. The educators inspire their students to embrace six sustainable happiness skills: gratitude, human connection, positive outlook, purpose, generosity and mindfulness.

Mr. Pramod Mahajan, M.Sc. (Physics), M.A. (Education), B.Ed. (Creativity), M.B.A. (Training & Development) Principal / School Director, Sharjah Indian School, Sharjah

KEEPING YOURSELF MOTIVATED IN THE CURRENT SCENARIO

It has been more than a year now that we are living amidst a very unpredictable and unimaginable time. It will not be wrong if I say that Covid-19 pandemic with its ever extending lockdown is a game changer as it brought a tremendous and overnight change in our working styles. As human beings, we are not used to adapting so quickly, and any such rapid change leads to anxiety , stress, depression and discomfort in many. We need to accept and understand now that when the game has changed we must empower ourselves with the required skill sets of the new game without any delay. We all must have our own 'Success Mantra' to keep us motivated to face the new normal.Our mind is an extraordinarily powerful thing. It is not just what makes us into us: the person that we are. It also has the power to make us into more than what we are, by helping us to motivate ourselves and to strive to achieve more, to learn and to develop. And it also has the power to make us less: for example, lack of self-belief. To remain self-motivated, we must look after our mind in every way just as looking after our body in terms of maintaining our overall health. There is more to keeping our mind healthy than simply eating well and exercising. Some form of self-reflection or meditation can be extremely helpful in maintaining a healthy balance in our mind. And I strongly believe that a healthy and balanced mind is the happy and motivated mind. Remember, positive thinking is the idea that can change our life. Research shows that positive thinking really does have a scientific basis. We can't change the world, but we can change how we perceive it and how we react to it. And that can change the way that we feel about ourselves and others, which can in turn have a huge effect on our overall well-being. Even current scenario of pandemic cannot affect positive and motivated people as they are resilient and mindful in all situations. We all will agree to the fact that working remotely/ work from home is more challenging during COVID-19 with extra stress and added distractions from family members.

I would like to share few simple strategies that are helpful in keeping us motivated and on task. Do not be too hard on yourself right now; we're all doing our best under these unprecedented circumstances. Just gain control over self, boost your own morale, never be a complainer, congratulate yourself on every small and big achievement, channelize your stress positively, be assertive, learn to relax, learn new skills and add on to the existing ones, meditate, exercise, remain self-motivated and keep your team motivated, socialize virtually, invest time in self-care and self-pleasure, have fun, laugh and practice mindfulness.

Mindfulness helps to halt the escalation of the negative thoughts associated with depression and teaches us to focus on the present moment, rather than reliving the past or being concerned about the future. When we are stressed, our negative thoughts and negative moods become intertwined and we get demotivated. There may be some areas where you either can't or don't want to change the situation. Your children may be happy and thriving in their hybrid approach in school and in your community. Your family may not have the money to uproot and move, even temporarily. Or maybe your organization has chosen to stay remote for a long time, and while that situation isn't ideal, you love the company and don't want to change jobs. In such cases, we need to accept our situation as it stands. Accepting what we can't change or what we're choosing not to change helps to make our situation feel less stressful because we're acknowledging our autonomy: 'I am choosing to stay in this job, to stay involved in this organization, or to continue to live in this city.' Once accepted, then we can find ways to make the situation more doable for us. Once we have questioned and observed everything in our environment, then we will need to develop a strategy for moving forward within these realities.

At times we may find it tough to stay on task and get our work done. To overcome this and feel motivated, we must create a schedule/ structured workday, establish a dedicated work place, dress formally, follow time schedule, challenge ourselves, reward ourselves, limit our distractions, feel good, experimenting with different strategies and practice regulating our emotions. This is an unusually challenging time worldwide. So let us keep ourselves motivated, exuding positive vibes in our environment and keep moving forward even when the times are tough. Let us use this situation as an opportunity to elevate our leadership to the next level and strive for excellence.

Dr Farzana Shakeel Ali is an Educationist and a Director-Principal at Kriti Public School, Barabanki, U.P.

With all the chaos happening around the world, uncertainty is the buzzing word. No one has a definite solution or direction to the problem. But there is one person who has something for you and that is YOU, yourself.

It is just you and your thought that will do the needful in the time of crisis. It is just one thought and the magic begins. Thought of being a unique self. At the end of the day you are the longest commitment. You are the most valuable investment.

At times when we are in a dark place we think we've been buried, but we've actually been planted. And never stop watering that sapling.

As this sapling is the magic tree that will produce fruits in future based on present habit and action.

So, be the best possible version of yourself, one tiny habit at a time. Be a consistent performer, no matter what may come.

So, let's begin the magic!

Dr. Raavee Tripathi, Principal, Sumitra Modern School, Sitapur, Uttar Pradesh

KEEPING YOURSELF MOTIVATED DURING THE PANDEMIC

Most of us are struggling to stick to healthy habits due to the current situation. There's less structure in our lives due to continuous transition from in-person to remote work and other challenges. Lot of us are facing additional stress and anxiety due to social isolation, financial worries, or family/personal health concerns. All of this makes it hard to stay motivated. Don't be too hard on yourself right now. We are all doing our best under these unprecedented circumstances.

A few simple strategies can keep you motivated and help you to cope and thrive during these challenging times. Important step towards regaining your energy is establishing a new daily routine. Try to get up at the same time every day. Have a plan for each day. Separate work hours from non-work activities. Without a structured workday, you might start shifting your work later in the day causing you to stay up later at night. Establish a time to begin and end work. Try to stick to it as much as you can.

Your bed is likely to be the most comfortable space in the house. But when you associate your bed with work, it can interfere with your sleep thereby affecting your performance the following day. Create a workspace somewhere else. Short periods of exercise help and often serve as motivation to exercise more. Practice healthy and mindful eating. Notice how good exercise makes you feel. Get sufficient rest. Relax and recharge. Give yourself small rewards when you accomplish a task or goal. Having something to look forward to makes it easier to stick to your plan when you're feeling a lack of motivation. If you are struggling with the habit of procrastination, start with small tasks. Motivation will likely increase when you experience progress, so get started with your task. Make a conscious effort to avoid distractions. When you work, silence your phone and ask people not to distract you. Keep contact with your supervisor and work colleagues. Assign specific times for activities like email and social media. Maintain your social interactions by talking to your friends and family regularly. Participate in online social activities. These are key for boosting your mood and energy.

It's okay to not be okay. Prioritize your mental health. Now might be a good time to learn some new relaxation techniques like mindfulness, yoga, and meditation. If news makes you nervous, reduce your exposure. Dealing with a range of emotions can quickly drain one's energy. Work on developing and maintaining a positive attitude. This can be hard when things seem bleak, and the future is uncertain. Be kind to yourself and acknowledge the difficult situation you are in. Maintaining your sense of humor is a good mood booster. A smile or laugh has healing effect on you as well as those who you interact with. Though this pandemic feels endless, it will eventually come to an end. The motivation tips that you adopt now can lead to positive changes for the rest of your life!

VINEETA KAPOOR, MA.Psy, PGDGC is a Psychologist and Counselor with 18+ years of experience is based at Canada and has enriched at Science of Wellbeing: Yale University and Conflict Management: University of California, USA

"Keeping oneself motivated in the present scenario..."

"Doing the best at this moment puts you in the best place for the next moment." - Oprah Winfrey

Covid-19 has proved to be one of the most devastating disease for humankind in the present century. It has powerfully impacted all generations and has taken away our loved ones, our belongings, our securities and it has left us in a state of trauma and shock . It feels, it's a nightmare, where we undergo hopelessness, helplessness and the only thing that could help us is to confront the given situations with the right state of mind. It has not only proved to be a health emergency but it has also caused economic and social disruptions where millions of people are left in abject poverty, all we can witness is the rising black smoke of the crematoriums, the loud sirens in the background and uncertainty regarding our lives. It is a period of constant fear and trauma. It is not only impacting our present but has significantly impacted our future too. The young innovative minds have lost their jobs, people are left with no resources yet every one of us has one thing which can prove to be the biggest resource which is our immense will-power and psychological strength. Covid is not only a battle of immunity or physical strength but it is a real difficult psychological battle. Our response towards the situation decides the consequences, if someone fails to recognize the power of their psychological strength then one is likely to fail prey to the disease.

Therefore, in the present time, our support system, our families, our well-wishers and the near & dear ones - have to prove to be our sole supporting pillars by providing constant unconditional support and assistance ... and taking care of oneself has become a priority in the current scenario. Though everything may seem to be gloomy and bleak but one can only come out of the storm when one knows how to navigate through it. Therefore, keeping oneself motivated is the need of the hour. Keeping oneself motivated in the dire situation may seem difficult but not impossible. Keeping oneself motivated not only yields positive result for oneself but also extends strength and positive vibes to others. We all can keep ourselves motivated through small things like maintaining routine which can help us to spend our time effectively and judiciously and help us to prioritize our work and find space for other leisure activities too. Apart from this, to manifest oneself one can practice yoga and meditation for both physical and psychological well-being, it can help us to relax from the core. Keeping in touch with our relatives, friends, colleagues is an important activity too as it gives us a sense of security and makes us feel protected. In the present time, many of us feel difficulty in expressing our thoughts and emotions but keeping a diary or a journal can help us to release our bottled-up emotions, seeking help from a professional can help too.

Keeping oneself positive and hopeful can prove to be the most efficient coping mechanisms. Distracting oneself from stressful information like avoid watching effecting news, taking frequent short breaks from social media can help us to maintain our wellbeing during the difficult time and lastly, one should realize, that everything is in our control – we are the remote control of ourselves , how do we respond to the situations, what type of approach we have towards the problem helps us to solve the most concrete issues, it is our internal locus of control, which can help us the most in the current scenario, and moreover one can only help others when oneself is motivated.

So Stay Strong ... Stay Positive ... & Never give up..

Jennifer Lobo, PGT Psychology, CCA Coordinator, a school principal at, H.G. International School, Rajasthan, India is a motivated and innovated facilitator. She is a professional, caring and organized educator with a period of 10 years of experience whose only commitment is to provide dedicated students with appropriate learning along with adventurous designed curriculum to fulfill their potential for spiritual, emotional, social, intellectual, psychological and physical growth.

KEEP YOURSELF MOTIVATED EVEN DURING THE CURRENT SCENARIO

"To every thing there is a season....

a time to keep silence, and a time to speak;
a time to love, and a time to hate;
a time for war, and a time for peace."

These sacred words from Holy Bible are truly the hallmark of the life we lead; where some are happy times, others sad; some are productive while others seem wasteful; some inspire peace and others bring pain. But all of them are necessary for us to learn, grow, and evolve. If we look closely enough, each experience reveals a greater purpose of our life as mortal.

In recent months, the news about the pandemic, economic woes and the uncertainty over what we can't control has triggered tremendous anxiety in the world around us but this flow of life is a process of change. We must acknowledge this process and move ahead with it. Sometimes the challenges we confront seem like dark tunnels, yet every tunnel has a light at the end of it.

Nothing in life is static for long and so is this pandemic. It is the need of the hour to cultivate positivity in our minds so that we can get through anything. Happiness is directly proportional to positivity we bring in our lives .It liberates our energy and inspires hopes.

When we reflect it is usually the hard times that provide us a new perspective. Though when in a crisis, we don't feel that way. But there are steps one can take to cope during difficult times and one must not forget that It is only in our darkest hours ,we may discover that the true strength lie ourselves and that can never, ever, be lowered . If we develop the habit of counting our blessings we can deeply realize the wonders of our life. Yet another way to feel blessed is by being kind to others , even when you are struggling,helping others can increase your positive feelings It has been truly heart warming to see how we all could touched upon each other's lives and felt more strength within us

One must be more mindful. When we live in present moment ,we stay away from the apprehension that the uncertain future brings along. One can develop the resilience to handle difficulties more easily, and bounce back more rapidly

We must practice gratitude i.e. an appreciation for the goodness in our life. This can be done by retrieving positive memories ,not taking things for granted as they come and by being hopeful and optimistic that there will be good things in future.Keeping a gratitude journal — writing down things we're thankful for — makes us more aware of when things go right.

Yet another useful way to be positive is train your mind to see the good things,infact in everything positivity is a choice the happiness of your life depends on the quality of your thoughts. Engage with the things that make you happy. No problem can halt your life and your happiness! Indulge in a hobby bit gardening, dancing, reading or listening to music

Several studies reveal that practicing yoga can lead to a decrease in symptoms of angst. It has proved to be an effective therapy for adverse circumstances. Meditation also relieves stress anxiety helps to gain a new perspective on stressful situations

If you Trust in God and your own inner Wisdom , you will find your paths radiating with hope and confidence

Don't forget to develop a support system ... a counselor, friends, family, or anyone with whom you can share your feelings and feel light hearted.

Take care of yourself ,Eat balanced diet exercise regularly; take plenty of rest.

Open up to what is happening and savour the good in your life

Concluding in the words of Martin Luther King, Jr. "We must accept finite disappointment, but we must never lose infinite hope."

Let us all pray and yearn for a new dawn where all the fears are conquered by our unflinching faith and courage.

Ms Jyoti Arora is the Principal at Mount Abu Public School, Rohini, Delhi. She is a proud recipient of National Teachers Award 2020. With over three decades experience in the field of education, love for children and the country, Ms Arora continuously strives for community welfare services through number of social initiatives.

Make Hay While the Sunshines

Last year in March 2020, COVID-19 was the worst thing that had happened to this generation! The unknown and uncertainty of the disease coupled with being stuck at home. Initially it felt like it would never end. After a week of wallowing in my misery I decided that I can make something positive of this gift of time that I have been given. Do all the hobbies and fun things that I had always wanted to do but never could find the time to do. Slowly I started making a list of all these activities and started fulfilling my long-lost desires. Read along to learn how I made hay while the world was healing.

Making Soap

I would watch videos of people making soaps and think to myself that seems easy enough! I can do that in an afternoon! Ironically, turns out, five years passed me by and I could never actually find that afternoon! So this was the first thing I started with in lock down. Making my own soap bars. It does actually just take an afternoon but deciding on the exciting things to put inside the soap takes much longer. Now I think I can call myself a pseudo-expert in soap making and finding the right ingredients that suit my skin.

Sharing the love

For years my daughters had been telling me to teach them many of our family recipes. But like everything else we could never find the time. During lockdown I was able to impart the wisdom that my mother had once with all her love endowed on me. After learning these recipes my daughters started a family Instagram page to share our creations –DecoyCreations. Go have a look and share our love for food with your family and friends.

Connecting Again

I graduated from St. Stephen's college many moons ago and could never really connect with many of friends. Lockdown taught all of us to slow down, reconnect and rekindle the friendships that once were. I feel grateful to the people who have touched my life in all these years.

Green thumb

I had always wanted a kitchen garden, from where I pluck fresh tulsi and have tulsi chai whenever my heart desired it instead of the packaged Ayurveda chai. During lockdown and after, I was able put strong roots down to have those treasured moments while I talk to my friends over zoom and remember the good old days.

Good Vibes

For years I have been doing mediation and pray for the health and wellbeing of any anyone I knew who was suffering and hurting. During lockdown I was able to connect with people like me. We would come together thrice a week to pray and heal those who were suffering. Being immersed in negative news all around us, this helped us feel positive and pray for those in need.

I hope these stories help you pass the 2021 lockdown and carpe diem!

Jyotsna Davar is an Educator with Directorate of Education, Govt of NCT, Delhi

KEEPING YOURSELF MOTIVATED DURING THE CURRENT SCENARIO

The sun rises and sets as usual. We are eating, drinking, sleeping with extra care. The epidemic has shattered the whole world. People are living in fear which has to be conquered. Tough times teach us lessons to the extent of change in personalities for better. Man can do his best to save, treat, live through and eradicate Covid 19. A time will come when we will live normal life. There is a gap but this can be filled with some best practices which one never found time to do. Discover your talents and nurture a hobby.

In 1971.. my husband Major Datt an Infantry officer was at front .. that time postman was the most awaited person on this earth. In 1999.... I remember sitting next to our landline phone waiting for a call from our son during the Kargil war.

Today, we are blessed with fastest modes of communication which bring you close in spite of being away. Connect with people you always wanted to but could not find time.

The creativity in form of art, poetry, comedy etc. is amazingly developing. Up-scale, learn new skills to energize you lifelong. Nothing better than a purpose to help people in need in form of material, financial, emotional and experience the joy of giving. Online apps can keep you busy.

Look ahead, when a baby is born one does think of his/ her future 15, 20 years ahead. When one start a business one looks ahead say 5 years from now ....there is always a vision.

Live with an attitude of gratitude.

A committed and disciplined educationist, Rama Datt is executive trustee, Maharaja Sawai Man Singh II Museum Trust, Jaigarh Public Charitable Trust, and Trustee, Shila Mata Temple Trust, in Jaipur, Rajasthan. In 37 years of experience she tried to make education easy, enjoyable and multidimensional at all levels.

Lesson from Crisis (Pandemic)

"Nothing in life is to be feared. It is only to be understood. Now is the time to understand more so that we may fear less."

Crisis like pandemics come to disrupt the normalcy of our lives and mould and push us by force into new ways of living. But if we look at history it tells us that these lessons do not last really long. Epidemiologists also over the world are bemoaning the fact that plagues of swine flu and Ebola etc could not teach us lasting lessons. That is why governments and public in general all have stayed in denial of Covid-19 for so long a time that a tiny virus mutated into the size of mammoth monster who claimed so many innocent lives all over the world. George Santayana wrote, "Those who cannot remember the past are condemned to repeat it." Let us stop denying the fact that we have to learn how to live with a virus that has infected millions. And remember the most important lessons covid-19 has taught us.

 # Personal Hygiene & the decluttering of our space at home and work place is not optional.

Learn the use of technology to the extent that you do not have to be present physically for every little domestic or official task.

Learn to differentiate between the real data and the fake news, which is spread to create panic & sensationalism.

Obey the rules and precautions for health safety.

Keep cash reserves to sail through the unexpected lockdowns.

Create and keep a routine to protect your sanity.

Acknowledge your feelings and share those with your loved ones. Keep the lives of positive communication open and active. Do not grieve alone. # Exercise for a better immunity.

And above all trust in the light at the end of the tunnel.

This Too Shall Pass.....

Archana Gaba is the Chief Learning Officer at Saint Kabir Gurukul Senior Secondary School, Jalalabad West, Punjab. She is a dynamic school leader with her footprints across globe in search of the holy grail of education. A trained NLP practitioner and Master Hypnotherapist by passion and an educator by profession, Archana Gaba has earned renown among counsellors and School Leaders.

In order to motivate yourself, *I think what you need to do is to create a goal that you really want to achieve with your passion.*

Something you are passionate about will always come easier to you. For example, it would be good to get some kind of certification or to master cooking.

I also think it is important to create several small, achievable goals rather than a big one out of the blue. With this pandemic, the world has shrunk, and it is now possible to connect with many people through zoom and other means.

This allows us to connect with like-minded people and take lessons online to achieve our goals. Information is important, but I recommend that you keep your reading of pandemic-related news to a minimum and use the time for yourself and your friends and families.

Nagi Ishihara is a professional working with General Affairs of HOPE Innovation Lab, Osaka, Japan.

The novel Coronavirus has been recognised *as the most destructive pandemic in the history of mankind, gripping the entire world in its fear and fatality. Ever since 'lockdown' has been implemented in the country, leaving us cooped up in our homes to eventually be complacent with the "new normal" phenomena, we have been experiencing things we once deeply wished for. And the reality has it that it took a pandemic to help us realise and live through them. Sigh!*

When was the last time you felt so connected to rest of the world? Never were all of humanity's concerns so aligned! For once, the world is thinking the same thoughts, sharing the same fears and battling the same enemy. We are all reaching for the same medicines and protective gear, and standing in queues for food, fearful for the next meal. Such synchronization would have been impossible to achieve ever! And yet today impossible is the new possible. Nobody is stronger than the other —the most powerful have fallen hardest to their knees. What the might of powerful nations, fear of a thousand armies, or the wisdom of a million saints could not have achieved, has been managed by a miniscule virus! Strange times indeed – life is being held to ransom by a non-living being, killing humans. This one instance convinces me God has a sense of humour too! We were all so cocksure of everything, uncaring about our environment, recklessly looting from the Earth that nurtured us, ungrateful for the love that surrounded us, isolating ourselves from fellow humans... In one fell swoop, a virus neutralized our negativity by pushing us into our homes. There has to be some meaning to all this, and we must understand the lessons this pandemic is teaching us......

Just trust the here and now; everything else can change in a matter of minutes! So what is power, money, big cars and big houses that we all cherish. Thus, live in the present and do not take experiences for granted. Appreciate life more – learn to value the small things(relationships, love and peace) talking to family and friends, something we are all doing now, but often gets neglected in everyday life. As individuals, we should be aware that this is the experience of a life-time, totally unique when we are all sailing the same boat. Even the two World Wars never brought the world to a halt, or on an even keel like this. So why are we competing with others all the time. What is the result, when we are all fighting for the same bed when corona strikes us. Ultimately God neutralise every thing on earth for us. So then why this jealousy, hate and anger ???

"LIFE'S A JOURNEY, NOT A RACE"

We live in a world that is constantly on the go—often at a breakneck pace. We are continually under pressure to be productive, to compete, and to never take a breather. While this mentality has its merits for producing various successes, it also has a way of wearing us down in every way possible. More specifically, it can be especially hard to enjoy the beauty of life if we're too busy racing through it. We are all one — and an individualistic point of view is not going to work. The rich are the same as the poor, the Europeans are the same as the Indians, the government is the same as the voters, the rulers are the same as the Opposition...we cannot overcome this pandemic unless we include everyone and watch out for each other.

Having said this, let's make our generation more loving and caring by introducing value education to children when young itself, rather than emphasising on marks / percentages, it is not the numbers that matter, but a good human being that we create who is filled with empathy towards society at large.

As communities and nations, we will have to use the present experience to be prepared for future conflicts and pandemics, some of which perhaps we cannot even imagine at present. It is important that we value the significance of scientific knowledge and the dangers of misinformation

Finally, Be grateful to COVID, it has taught us life, about ourselves.....this is when can think about our great Bharat, "Atmanirbhar Bharat"

Lastly my pen tends to bleed as I write this....If words can heal I can write nonstop.....

Amita Pandit Bhatt is a Founder of Educantum.inc, Mumbai, and the Director Principal at Asheville World School, Mumbai, Maharashtra

Keeping yourself motivated even during the current scenario

It was a huge challenge to keep our self motivated during lockdown and Covid period. Ever since lockdown started in March 2020, atmosphere around was depressing and gloomy. We were house arrested and confined to our home. We were never used to such preventive custody for such a long period. It was a tough phase for all of us to cope up with. First month was the most difficult period, when we all were trying to adjust with newly imposed situation. We were not only upset but depressed also.

It was a unique challenge for us which we had never faced earlier in life. In the changed circumstances I started exploring the ways which may keep motivating me even during this time of crisis. After giving much thought, I developed following points, which helped me a lot to keep myself constructively occupied in various productive activities and motivated me to do my job with zeal and enthusiasm.

Scheduled virtual get together with friends & relatives

Since we were totally cut off from outer world, I made it a point to be part of scheduled virtual meetings / get together with friends / relatives. This exercise kept me in touch with close friends & relatives and provided much needed moral support.

Priority to maintain Mental & Physical Health

During this period, priority was to enhance immunity of body. It was possible through exercise & nutritious food. I have been doing yoga exercises, breathing exercises and pranayama on daily basis. It not only kept me fit and healthy but also helped to fight with challenges of Corona. We also avoided outside food and had home cooked nutritious food only.

Carve out time for honing hobbies

During usual time it was not possible for me to devote enough time for my hobbies. During this period I managed to satisfy my inner soul by honing my hobbies – gardening, listening to music and reading books.

Learning New Technology and using it

I am not very tech-savvy person. During Corona period every activity is being organized virtually. Hence I learned to use technology as per requirement of the day and attended / organized endless webinars and virtual meetings. It boosted my confidence level and helped me to connect with others almost on daily basis.

More time for family

It was the golden opportunity to have healthy interactions with family. I had several discussions on different topics with my children. We not only interacted but played various indoor games, which was almost impossible during usual days. Proximity with family transformed the home into a healthy & joyful zone.

Completing Pending Work

During usual days in spite of my best efforts, few work would always remain unattended. Corona period gave time to complete the pending work and to do planning for future ventures.

Learning New Skills

During this period I also learnt few new skills. Culinary Art is one of them. I tried 'hands on practice' to cook vegetables and daals. Through this new skill I contributed my bit in cooking food at home.

Love with Literature

This unusual phase provided me time to express my thoughts in the form of write ups and poems. I wrote around 20 articles and 50 poems on various aspects of life. It satisfied my literary thirst.

Above activities kept me constructively occupied and motivated me to pass this crucial time with zeal and good spirit. These activities helped me to maintain mental and physical health well and kept the depression away.

Sanjay Bhartiya is the Principal of Nav Bharti Public School, Deepali, Pitampura, Delhi. He is also the Vice President of the Action Committee of the Unaided Recognised Private Schools and the Patron of the Forum of Public Schools, Delhi

Social distancing, masks, sanitizing to the extent of a certified OCD, *locked up in our houses and so many other such depressing things: Last year and current year have literally gone against the very grain of normal behavior* *humans have known. After all we were social animals. People around the world are reaching breaking points. Closed schools, work from homes, closing businesses and isolation for months together - we cannot take it anymore is the common refrain. After months of being stuck inside, limited exposure to friends and family, and juggling responsibilities at home and at work, it's no surprise that many of us are dealing with frustration, anger, and more. Putting us under a tremendous amount of stress, increasing our responsibilities, and stripping us of our support networks, this epidemic has proved to be a perfect recipe for burnout and breakdown. But we have a choice.*

We can succumb to the pressure and give up, or we can rally and fight for our career, our life, and our mental health. If we choose the first option, there is a guaranteed failure. The second option, though, will give us the opportunity to innovate, to succeed, and to grow stronger through what you overcome. In psychology, the acceptance paradox is that when we accept what we are truly feeling, those emotions then have less power over us — not more. Once we have questioned everything in our environment, then we will need to develop a strategy for moving forward within these realities.

The new normal needs new methods as well. For example, what would have been a simple walk to the desk and talk solution, might need a more organized call over digital channel.

But with little ingenuity applied, the digital channel could be as productive as a walk to the desk. We should cultivate few habits to avoid the classic "Learned Helplessness".

Little bit of exercising, reading, being outside, doing a creative hobby, connecting with family and friends, praying, writing, journaling, going to a religious service, and listening to music; these simple activities help us to avoid the feeling "No matter what I do I can't improve my situation".

Feeling anger, questioning what is possible, accepting what isn't changing and developing a strategy to move forward – we need some applied thought and action to handle these challenges. And, In the end we need to invest in some selfcare.

We all deserve it. Stay motivated and keep moving forward even when times are tough.

Dr. Sangeeta Bhatia, Principal, KIIT WORLD SCHOOL, PITAMPURA, DELHI. She is an alumnus of Miranda House for graduation and Masters with first class, P.hD. in bio inorganic chemistry from Delhi University, UGC NET qualified in 1984. Recipient of Fellowship from UGC as well as Department of Atomic Energy, BARC, Senior under officer, NCC, participated in RD parade of 1989 at Rajpath Joined KIIT 35 years ago and have been engaged in raising self reliant, Global Indian Citizens who have a passion for learning for life while collaborating with others to improve quality of life for mankind. She is a Recipient of National Teachers Award 2008, Cbse teachers award 2004, State teachers award 2003 and has been an Ex chairperson North West Delhi sahodaya complex, Vice president DSSTF, Member Governing Body, CBSE, Member, Governing Body RPVV, GNCT, Delhi, Published 14 research papers in International journals of repute, Various papers presented and published in conferences India and abroad and is a Master trainer for CBSE and GNCT, Delhi.

Keeping Yourself Motivated Even during the Current Scenario.

Principals have an arduous career as a school leader, responsible for students, staff, and parents. Their days are filled with heaps of paperwork and answering dozens of phones calls apart from meeting people, replying to emails, and WhatsApp messages. Everyone comes with a problem seeking an instant solution and the Principal is relegated to a good firefighter dousing fire.

The time management skills are stretched to the max. I am sure all my colleagues can relate to it. In addition to anxiety, Pandemic added some more emotions-overwhelmed, sadness, stress, frustration, uncertainty, and worries. Even before the pandemic, principals were facing unprecedented levels of accountability pressure and other stressors. The toll of the Pandemic was palpable.

Much of the focus has been put on the students' social emotional wellbeing, mental health of the teachers and teacher burnout issues but the pressures of long hours and coping up with the challenges of dealing with uncertainties mounts up on the school leaders too.

School leaders do not generally talk about their mental health, as they are role models. They do not want to be judged. Their ability to manage their emotions is an indicator how teachers feel.

A school leader is expected to provide tangible or intangible extrinsic motivation to the staff, more intangible during Covid time- in the form of encouragement and appreciation but must remain intrinsically motivated all the time.

During the current scenario, the students had to be connected to learning; teachers had to be given lessons in digital literacy; adverse circumstances had to be transformed into opportunities for growth and success. Engaging and involving myself with the task at hand, thereby remaining occupied 24/7 where was the time to get frustrated?

Virtual meetings skyrocketed, contributing to Zoom fatigue. It is a good thing for remote communication but just because we can use it does not mean we have to. Realizing this Zoom calls and meetings were reduced, giving everyone the much-needed relief.

Long sitting hours without any movement resulted in writing a slogan "Be mobile with mobile." With every ring now I get up and walk in the room for some physical activity.

Working in a foreign country brings its own set of challenges. Supporting the community during tough times feels satisfying.

Principalship is isolating; more so if you are WFH. So, finding your tribe helps you to connect, collaborate and share. I am fortunate to be a part of a very cohesive group- Oman Chapter- where all of us connected and found support. "We were in the same storm".

Creating a dedicated workspace has a lot of benefits. It allows you to focus and mentally gets you into work. Mine has aromatic candles and diffuser with lemon grass oil. It is refreshing and relaxing.

We were thrown into a situation we never anticipated, and it did change my natural sleep pattern. A voracious reader has no difficulty.

It is the inner drive which pushes me to go on, successfully completing one project and moving on to the next. I am sure my fellow principals too have that drive, as they want to, not because someone told them to.

Were there moments of helplessness? Yes, when I had to console my colleagues, offering support to a grieving team member over the loss of their near and dear ones in India. No flights, phone funerals. My heart ached.

It is of paramount importance to recognize the stressors and try to address them. We must reflect and develop personal strategies to be resilient.

Sanchita Verma is a Principal at Indian School, Sohar, Sultanate of Oman. A merit holder in Zoology Masters as well as in B.Ed, and M.Ed Mrs. Sanchita Verma has a rich experience of over 35 years in education. She has held various positions as a college lecturer, head of the department, academic coordinator and principal in prestigious schools in India and abroad. As Principal Indian School Sohar, Oman since August 2012, she has proven herself as an asset to the Indian community in Sohar with her dynamic leadership, astute planning and academic cum administrative acumen with astounding inter-personal relationship.

Motivation. A simple word, yet with so much *depth that leads to more and more complex tributaries of thoughts once we try to delve into its understanding. So to have motivation, one must have an aim in life. In a routine life where one's week of work is all set in our phone's calendar, when yearly goals are already set in stone and when personal targets are tinged with a material chime; it is most obvious that any sudden change will rattle any modicum of motivation in every person. Indeed, the current pandemic has changed the traditional ways of doing things. People are currently facing traumatic experiences and a lot of stress. The prevailing uncertainties, sadness and depression are directly or indirectly causing untold harm to our emotional well-being and are reasons for losing our motivation and focus in life. We have become somewhat helpless during the present situation but what becomes more significant is to keep ourselves motivated.*

The pandemic came in a global wave of adjustment where all repetitive ways of life went out of the window. As this sea of change washed away all usual ways of living amidst a mist of uncertainty and a prison-like lockdown forced by an invisible enemy, one can only wonder, where our objectives in life went. A new term sprang from the turmoil that touched nearly all countries of the world, with India and the US the most affected, which is "the new normal". This begs the question, what is that new normal?

Funny are the ways of fear, as is it exactly fear that changed our world, fear of a virus, fear of the unknown, fear of our own species carrier of this new virus. And surely, it is this fear-plagued mind and not the pandemic that rattled the ways of motivation and made us forget a lesson learnt many a time along the centuries. The human race already encountered several global calamities. The Spanish flu, polio, world wars and countless others have been so much worse than the current pandemic. Yet we did come through stronger, with motivation our weapon of choice the key being fearlessness. The important thing is how we direct our motivation and so what is our motive? The answer has a psychological bearing where adopting a positive attitude and philosophy of life becomes important. And surprisingly enough, it could be that the Covid

19 itself could be the trigger to our motivation. We have for too long a time lived like robots, meeting ends and watching time fly by. There is a need for a deeper travel into our own psyche, find our own aims in life far from the materialistic world and ask the right questions. We need to focus on our emotional well-being and find ways to keep mental state healthy. Sharing positive vibes among peers and family members could definitely help fight against boredom and a restricted routine. Likewise, embracing new challenges and innovation might also be one of the means to maintain that motivation. This can also be achieved by transforming challenges into opportunities.

This new normal image brought to us by Covid 19 also brought with it new challenges and lost ways of life as well. We got to be more open to each other, talk about true things in life, lockdown keeping families closer, more time we got to spend with our children, appreciating the little things in life, appreciating things that we took for granted, the value of a meal's worth, of agriculture and of our basic needs. Out of fear, some went to fight for toilet paper, but with motivation to cut this fear loose, the power of humanity can help each other in these trying times. As long as we keep our motive and aim to be the betterment of humanity as a whole, motivation will never be that hard a quest. Instead of running away from understanding,

Covid 19 as a great teacher could have been just the eye opener humanity has for so long sought with closed eyes. The only thing that is required is true motivation to meet a positive destiny, and this remains very much in our own hands.

As Buddha rightly said: "If you want to fly, give up anything that weighs you down." So, all stakeholders can work together to keep the motivation level high to confidently face current situations.

Shimla Hemraj, BA, PGCE, MBA, is an Educator in English since 2003 in Mauritius.

Covid 19 has impacted people in various ways as a result of which there is increase of fear, anxiety and concern level.

To keep yourself motivated most important limit your exposure to media coverage, create and maintain a daily routine of the theory of 8 +8+8, which is the balance system of life to keep yourself motivated in any situation of your life. Each day you have twenty four hours, it should be well distributed in three parts. first eight hours of your day should be honest and ethical hardwork in your profession or studies. second eight hours should be a good sleep or a power nap or rest. third eight hours of the day are very important to win your life and keep yourself motivated. if you fail in the third eight hours, you lose your life and yourself. third eight is 3 F, 3 H and 3 S- Family, friends and faith in god -Connect with family and friends and have faith in God.

Health, hygiene and hobby- take care of your health and heigene and not miss out on your hobbies, service, soul, smile and if you want to serve the society, always do so with a smile. The 3F, 3H and 3S should consume atleast eight hours of your day to keep a balanced life and keep yourself motivated. if you equally divide your time in all the nine departments you will lead an optimistic and a balanced life.

Ms Rachna Bhimrajka, the founder of FUN2LEARN is a dynamic, innovative, dedicated and a focused endupreneur for more than one & a half decade. She conducts handwriting and several skills development programs. She is also curriculum designer of handwriting, vedic maths and abacus and is based at Mumbai, India.

This global predicament has made us reflect upon how uncertain life can be.... But at the same time it has also made us realize the immense human power to deal with such uncertainties. Since such a massive pandemic situation happened to all of us for the first time, none of us was trained to handle this. So we had to find out our own ways to keep our motivation, hope and productivity intact. Being a leader, it was even more imperative for us to be inspiring for our teams as well as the students as they were all looking up to us as to how we deal with this new challenge. As an educator, our first and foremost responsibility is to safeguard our students from any kind of threat to their intellectual and emotional well being. The only way was to engage them into joyful learning activities so the situation could not get better of them. Our absolute focus on finding innovative ways to keep our students actively engaged in online learning experiences, has been keeping us highly satisfied. There are few tips that I have been sharing with my team of warriors to keep them energized so that they are able to deal with the current situation. These activities worked out really well for me to remain holistically active during this challenging time.

Morning workout- Make sure that minimum 30 minutes are exclusively dedicated to morning physical fitness regime that comprises Suryanamaskar, other stretching exercises and few breathing exercises. In addition to this, a few minutes of meditation will help you explore you inner self and gives you clarity of thought process. This keeps you charged up throughout the day.

For keeping your cognitive faculties active, make sure that you keep researching and finding out new ideas and strategies to be implemented on everyday basis so that the students also feel excited and motivated to incorporate creativity into their day to day learning process.

This pandemic lockdown has also given us a chance to come closer to our families. With no household help to our aid, we are getting a chance to try new recipes and cook for our homefolks. Assigning work to all the family members and witnessing everyone taking the responsibility, keeps the mind active. Spending quality time with your own children will give you a different level of emotional satisfaction.

Even to check on the well being of friends and dear ones, sharing the vows of the downtrodden, finding new ways of helping out people, is keeping us socially active.

Then the evenings can be spent giving time to our long lost hobbies like listening to music or dancing or playing with pets. The idea is to stay as occupied as we can so that we can make use every bit of this time available to us. The skills which will keep us going are adaptability and agility. Let's sharpen these new age skills and gear up for the fast changing world.

Dr. Archna Sharma is a school principal who strongly believes that creativity is an inherent quality of each and every child that must be revitalized and honed. She attained her Ph.D in management on the topic 'TQM in Secondary School Education' and is a mission oriented, focused and an educator of eminence as Principal in various Army Schools and other CBSE schools pan India. Presently she is the principal of ORCHIDS The International School, Malad branch in Mumbai. She has been conducting training workshops for teachers and students on various issues related to effective teaching & learning strategies, soft skill development, and student empowerment.

"Live Life to the Fullest Without Conditions"

I know things look bleak right now. You're lonely, down in the dumps, and it feels like this heaviness will weigh you down forever. We all are going through these rough conditions.

"I can't do this anymore" - a common message that reverberates among people around the world: Enough of being inside. Enough of working remotely. Enough of having businesses shut down. Enough of schools being closed. Enough of being isolated. Enough of everything. The patience and hope are gone. It's natural to get furious about what's taking place right now. And it's important to respond and express that

resentment in healthy ways.

But giving up and becoming hopeless will not bring tranquillity to us or resolve everything. Remember that emotions are guests. They come and they go.

This mountain of uncertainty, hopelessness and impatience that we carry with us is burdening us. Let's try and move on from it, together.

You have two choices: either you give up or you wake up, look at the brighter side and inspire everybody.

We need to stay motivated and encourage others to be the same. Being motivated helps keep your mind and body robust. By being hopeful, you're surrounding yourself with an aura of positivity and strength and you will feel revitalized. Positive thinking helps with stress management and can indeed enhance your overall health. When you're optimistic, you'll feel better about life. It's impractical to feel positive and negative at the same moment—and alacrity is contagious- so the more confident you are, the more joyful emotions you have. You'll feel more harmonious, livelier and relaxed. When you have less stress and concerns in your life, you have extra energy to do the tasks you prefer- like being dynamic and fit. Sometimes our mind is the reason for our lethargy. Stressing and worrying incessantly can prevent one from looking at the happier part of life, whilst draining our energy and vigour. We feel annoyed, moody, and uninterested in the things we admire. Energize yourself by simply changing your perspective!

A positive state of mind creates positive sentiments. Positive emotions create a positive lifestyle. What would you rather be? Happy all the time or constantly angry?

Just like every other challenging time in history, this time will pass too, and we will bounce back. In the meantime, it is important to keep ourselves motivated and enthusiastic.

The situation is severe, and it is tough for us to stay motivated at all times but there are several methods available to stay motivated and have a positive attitude.

Our recommendation is the four F rule—Feel, Face, Focus and Fight to use everything that's happening to you right now as an opportunity to become a more resilient person. At first, feel your emotions: anger, frustration, disgust, etc. Then face your current situation and all your shortcomings and complaints. Next, focus on the future and set your goals. Lastly but most importantly, fight back everything coming your way to achieve goals you have set for yourself.

So, instead of being crushed down by the weight of it all, approach life with a sense of hope and tenacity that motivates you to not only get through — but also thrive. See the good in the bad and try knowing yourself on the inside. Do what you aspire to do and make notable progress. Everyone is going through this problematic phase of life together. Life isn't without its share of ups and downs, thus, stop thinking and start doing what you wish to do, for as the saying goes "Live as if you have no tomorrow, and every day will become the most beautiful present....."

Dr Sreya Chattopadhyay is a technopreneur with a doctoral degree in Health care Management. Currently she is working on Data analysis and Artificial Intelligence. She also runs a NGO, AHCF, which helps the adolescents and ladies of this country towards development of their better health and mind. Her NGO works with doctors from around the world not only to help common people but also to help the doctors to network and learn from each other. She is based in Delhi.

"ASPIRE TO INSPIRE YOURSELF BEFORE YOU EXPIRE"

This adage itself inspired me a lot. As we know that death is as sure as tax... so why not lead a self-motivated life during the pandemic.

I was myself infected along with other 5 family members. Thus there was no necessity to isolate. We religiously followed the COMBO MEDICINES and took other precautionary measures. We were fortunate enough to recover by taking care of each other during that period.

I would like to share few activities which gave me the inner strength to get rid of the PHOBIA tagged with this pandemic. Though it was not a bed of roses to do so ::

TOTALLY avoided seeing the negatives on social & print media;

I never gave up on my daily exercise and meditation, though it was difficult because of physical weakness. I stuck to my half-an-hour Anulom Vilom (Lungs), Bhastrika Pranayaam (Lungs), Kapaalbhati (Stomach), Brahmi (Mind), etc., etc;

I stayed connected with friends and foes. Enjoyed HR (Human Relationship) through phone calls and other connecting facilities available.

Rabindranath Tagore has rightly said that :

"Alone I can 'ENJOY' but together we can "CELEBRATE"

"Alone I can 'SMILE' but together we can "LAUGH";

Utilized each precious moments at home to get my book published. This was my debut effort :: " 100 TEN COMMANDMENTS for EDUCATORS";

Never forgot my FAMILY PRAYER to bless all infected persons in family, neighborhood, country and our globe;

Terrace Gardening took majority of my time;Encouraged like-minded people in the colony to buy an Oxygen Cylinder on a pooled contributory basis. Now the cylinder can be used by these 9 members , as and when, required;

Counseled many infected friends, on request, of course. Shared with them what precautions to take and how to remain cool during the PANDEMIC times;

For self-pacification distributed grains and other utilities to 15 needy families;

As per convenient time ... took care (fed) of stray animals ... dogs, cows, etc.

Dr. Clarence Peter is a former school Principal, a Soft Skills Guru, an Edu Consultant and an Author based at Patna in Bihar.

"This too shall pass" *has been my mantra during these uncertain and challenging Covid times. Last year in 2020 the country wide lockdown was imposed to handle the Covid situation very close to my birthday. For me the* *most immediate upsetting thing was that I wouldn't be able to be with my family to celebrate it as I was Principal in a school 300 km away from my hometown. Least did I imagine that it is just the start of a year full of challenges. As captain of the ship my first challenge was to make my team shift to virtual environment and adopt new approaches for teaching students which were really an uphill task for them.*

As the months passed by the big question remained when would schools reopen and resume classes in physical mode. Safety from virus was indeed prime but educators had to face a bigger worry - how will they cover up the learning gap that is gradually widening due to online learning. With the cases still on surge, the light at the end of the tunnel remains distant.

But at the same time, I feel blessed being in a profession where we teachers are contributing no less than the frontline covid warriors. As the scenario changed, it got clear that the virtual classrooms are going to stay for at least sometime. Evaluating the gravity of the situation, me and my team pledged to connect with children by caring about them first, and teaching them next. This commitment was a great motivating factor for me during these pandemic times. We pepped up our classes with positive affirmations, praise, virtual rewards and certificates of appreciations. We stayed flexible as best we could, and organized online Smile and Joy hours and active circle time. I tried to virtually interact with children, hold on demand sessions with them as much as possible. This helped me build bonds and create beautiful connects as well as I did not have to miss the smiles and cheer that children naturally bring in with their presence. Top of all it helped a lot in keeping my faith alive and in place.

Other thing that kept me motivated was the great opportunity to learn and read. I attended various online sessions, enrolled myself in open learning courses, conducted and moderated webinars and workshops. The best part was that I could take time out to brush off the dust from the books that were in my 'To Read List' for months (and some even for years) but due to busy schedule everyday it was not possible for me to enjoy their company. As P B Shelley said "If Winter comes, can Spring be far behind" indeed the strong faith that these days are not going to last forever and this new normal is by all means soon going to give way to the real normal, is biggest of all motivations. So, let's all pray for the same and keep our fingers crossed!

Neha Sharma, Principal Gd Goenka Ghaziabad: An educator by choice Neha, is currently working as Principal at G D Goenka Public School Ghaziabad. She has been working for promoting life-skills for children as an educator, school leader and also as a policy maker. She has worked with CBSE as Deputy Secretary (2012-19) before joining back the school domain. She has been an Author/ Co-Author for 50 + CBSE publications: Life Skills Manuals, CCE Manuals, Gender Sensitive Pedagogy Manuals, CBSE-International Curriculum, SQAA, Values Education etc, to name some.

"Keeping yourself motivated even during the current Scenario"

"No matter how dark it is right now,

Remember that the battle will end,

The Sun will rise and you will find your joy again"

-Winnie Mathenge

The human spirit cannot be contained for a very long time in a state of limbo and inaction. Human beings are also named as social animals hence they used this time as an opportunity to connect and rediscover themselves.

The blessing in disguise is the time that we can spend with the family (sans the gadgets). It's important to know about one's roots. Our family history, it's origin it's journey through generations. Constructing and documenting the family tree is very important as it gives us an insight into our ancestors' way of life and knowledge about their struggles, triumphs and tribulations. This can be a beneficial learning resource for the next generation. Because this will also inculcate a sense of gratitude as well as hope amongst us besides giving us an understanding of human nature and psychology. We will be more rooted in human values.

Our main Dharma in life as a human is to find happiness in every moment. How can we do this? First of all try to stay cheerful and positive, complain less, instead of instant gratification look for the opportunities for making judicious use of available resources by learning how to differentiate between our needs and desires. Acceptance and adaptability to every given situation builds resilience in human beings. All these are the most essential 21st century skills.

We can also be happy by pursuing something which we always liked and wanted to but avoided indulging in, finding some excuse or the other, most common among them lamenting about shortage of time. Pursuing a hobby or learning new skills is always a happy pastime as it imbues self-confidence and opens new vistas of opportunities relevant for happy human existence. Therefore family time for the following will build-on the emotional connect and will also inculcate a certain desired level of discipline among young and old alike. Prayer, play, exercise for physical fitness, reading and cooking and sharing the household chores together can be big stress busters. Besides these can also strengthen bonding amongst the family members. Reading and writing enhance one's imagination, creativity and language skills which are important soft skills. Cooking is an important life skill, a step towards independence. It's an exhilarating feeling when you are not dependent on anyone to satiate your small needs.

Gratitude, kindness and being useful to society is another important aspect of human existence. Find out how we can be helpful to someone in need? We can join a self-help group or an NGO that works with people in need. And please do not term it as charity because we would like to do this to help ourselves. Being useful to another human being is an opportunity very few get hence if you find peace and satisfaction in such work only then get involved and be grateful.

For every human endeavor one needs intrinsic motivation. Listening to your heart, your inner voice and then pursuing whatever makes you happy at the same time is beneficial for you in the longer run. Extrinsic motivation does not make a lasting impact, we just get involved in some pursuits for a short period of time and then feel dejected about the whole thing as it doesn't satiate our souls.

Leaving aside our bias and overlooking individual differences and inequalities of religion caste, creed, gender, social stature, abilities looking at the ways of hand holding and supporting each other. By creating a sense of Universal Brotherhood only can sail us through the Tsunami of fear, disease and endless misery and give a ray of hope to humanity also a chance to reinvent itself.

Kalpana Chaudhary, a TEACHER by choice. In classrooms from 1972. People's person! A lifelong learner who is passionate about progressive, inclusive, joyful and equitable education. Has set up and nurtured three CBSE schools in South Gujarat. Currently working as the Director Emeritus at N.H.Goel World School, Raipur which she has set up and nurtured.

Covid 19 pandemic took us unawares, *when the wave silently entered the Indian States and created an uproar. For us educators it was that time of the year when we were all busy with planning and conducting exams in schools. Children were already in a state of panic as they were preparing for the year end exams while parents were busy doing the impossible ie make their children sit down to study. Never had mankind received a jolt of this degree and terrified into being secluded to this level. By the time the news about the first slew of covid cases came to everyone's notice it had already become a Horror Story. News went around about how this is an untreatable and uncurable disease. People started panicking and within a matter of days the government announced complete lockdown and closed down everything which one would never have expected. We were well into the last week of March 2020 when postponement of exams was announced. Everyone was in house arrest and not before many months passed in the same state, did we all come to know the monstrousness and delinquency of the novel corona virus that had struck the world.*

The worst fear was that here was no cure at hand and it would take long scientific researches to have a verified treatment to save lives. Not only was everyone faced with utter fear about falling prey to the disease but many were doomed to experience psychological stress and fear. This was as true for young children as it was for grown up, middle aged and older people who used to be busy throughout the days. For months together we all waited for the disease to miraculously stop and medical fraternity to control it, but nothing of that sort happened. Slowly by August 2020 the wave started dropping, and as the number of infected people reduced, so did the casual attitude of the people increase. So, while the guidelines of covid still kept going around and the doctors and medical fraternity still kept advising and requesting people to follow the safety protocol, there were hundreds of people who did not bother. As the year 2020 was ending, things seemed better, hence even people with best intentions felt that safety protocols can be released.

January to March 2021 saw not just the layman but the government also commit blunders, like organising and participating in crowded events which were religious in nature or political in nature. Not being able to identify the larger and bigger silent wave which was raising its ugly fatal head, growing up until it burst at its seams! March end 2021 brought with it infections in masses when every third person was talking about fatal end of patients and the sad state of their families who were unable to cope up with tragic unexpected loss of dear ones. One thing was clear to everyone now, that there was no certainty about how this wave will peak and finish. People came to understand that safety protocols will have to be distinctly continued and followed seriously. Any activity which led to crowding had to be strictly contained or stopped whether it was business or marketing, or even activities which were really important for sustaining life for more than half the population.

Schools definitely were the last priority and so they remained shut. One big reason being, the government never wanted to take the risk of opening the schools and which would have sent parents clamouring to courts and administration citing safety protocols. Another conclusion was that the administration probably thought school education if lost will not make much of a difference. The parents were unsure hence did not want to take the risk of sending children to schools though they were happy sending them out to play because they probably couldn't handle them at home. Those who followed the guidelines and also inspired others to do the same, not just to save themselves but to save their precious near and dear ones, were less in number. There were those who were casual themselves and discouraged their own family and friends from following the protocol calling them cowards, despite seeing the disaster unfold. It is a matter of utter shame that some people didn't respect even the medical fraternity who bent backwards trying to save precious lives.

People realised how an important human trait, ie to interact and enjoy others' company turned into that of fear, meeting anybody was a terror now! They realised causing or inflicting disease and pain on family and friends is not what they wanted, hence not just to save themselves, often to save others, they imposed restriction of not going out to meeting anyone. There were occasions when in their darkest and most painful times of losing precious loved ones, family and friends were not able to join and support them in these dreadful times.

Another learning that Covid 19 brought in was that since the virus did not have any immediate cure it became imperative for researchers to go on working in such disastrous conditions. Researchers and medical fraternity became the frontline workers besides the other communities of service providers like the guards, cleaners, the law-keepers etc, so it was very important for the general public to understand how in such trying times, these people were delivering and performing their regular duties. Finally, researches led to discovery of new vaccines, indigenous as well as *foreign, and they were produced in large scale. But the irony was that people did not want to take the vaccines considering this to be a sham. By the time people did comprehend that the only cure was vaccine, they were confronted with the second wave of the lethal mutant virus spreading like wild fire in April 2021. Now everyone wanted to take the vaccine. By his time the vaccine was either wasted in large numbers or sufficient vaccine was not available.*

A bigger learning is for administrators, that a proper follow up of research should have been done. Complete groundwork to deal with this disaster was not done, in spite of being one of the largest populated countries. Events which could have been avoided, continued to transpire whether it was flocking in religious congregations, arranging large political rallies, or holding the IPL. My thoughts run berserk when I start recounting the kind of horrors that this year has shown us and everyone around, and my thoughts become incoherent! Of course, one of the biggest loss I feel, is the forfeiture of 360-degree holistic development of children where brakes were applied in the past year. We must brace ourselves to deal with not just stories of pain and loss, but also be equipped to endure weakened physical, mental and emotional health of the masses as well!

Amita Saxena is the Former Principal of DPS Sushant Lok, Gurgaon, a passionate educationist with 25 years rich experience in prestigious schools of Delhi NCR. Conferred with several awards including the prestigious Delhi State Teachers' Award 2016 and CBSE Teachers' Award 2019. Has worked ardently towards creating happy schools, collaboration and spreading environmental awareness.

Hopes, dreams, aspirations... *everything came to a halt. The year 2020 arrived with fear and uncertainty all around. COVID-19 left a deep physical, emotional, psychological, social and economic scar which will take years to heal. It has impacted the lives of millions across the globe. The pandemic has unmasked all claims of medical and scientific developments. COVID-19 is a warning bell – that despite of all our scientific claims and achievements, we are not prepared to handle a pandemic, we urgently need to invest in building strong health care system. Although the pandemics do not last forever but it certainly gives life lessons and opportunities to look back and ponder and reset our priorities.*

A year ago, we wouldn't have in our wildest dream imagines that wearing mask, social distancing, virtual communication, etc. will become a way of life. As we say every cloud has a silver lining. While COVID-19 has given rise to numerous challenges it has also yielded some valuable lessons.

Adaptability to the new normal. Maintaining social distance and using technology to work from home, virtual gatherings, online teaching and learning, all this has ensured a sense of normalcy in the otherwise dismal and depressing situation. A swift shift to the digital platform has become the order of the day

The pandemic has taught us to prioritize our relationships with family and friends. This most crucial time has given us an opportunity to work upon interpersonal relationships, to reconnect and rebond with those who matter. To value relationships is one essential lesson we learnt during this unfortunate time of our life.

"Live today as if there is no tomorrow." This is one of the hardest but the most practical lessons learnt. We need to learn to live in present. Too much of mad rush to accumulate wealth, to win that race to succeed in career etc. has actually made our lives lonelier and

deprived of all happiness, love and care of our family and friends. We are merely existing not living. Ironically, COVID has taught us this in the hardest way possible.

The past year set me thinking how much we fretted about the most trivial issues. But how little we need to live, to survive. We did not go to the malls, theatres, restaurants or holidays but we sailed through, we lived comfortably in the security of our homes in the company of our family who is our world.

COVID taught us to love and care our own self. Our health and wellness is most important. Maintaining hygiene and cleanliness, exercise, meditation, eating healthy is important. The pandemic has resulted in a desire to learn Yoga, meditation, developing a hobby etc. with an intention to cope up with stress.

Finally, we need to open our eyes to what the climate protagonists have been screaming about but we have been ignoring. Humans are living well beyond the natural boundaries. If we still do not stop messing with nature and continue with our high polluting way, then we may dodge the pandemic for now but we will still be in constant risk.

Pooja Sehgal is Principal of Kanya Kubja Public School, Kanpur, COE, CBSE District Training Coordinator (Kanpur & Unnao), CTET City Coordinator, Kanpur and a Subject Expert of English.

There are certain phases in the vicissitudinous journey of our lives which are the test of our resilience and equanimity, our love and empathy and most significantly, our faith and fortitude.

As we witness the lethal surge of the pandemic overwhelming mankind with pain, suffering and grief, we cannot help feeling traumatized and devastated- this is one such are situation which is largely beyond our control and our first response should be to accept it as such and keep our faith steady and strong. The best way to do this and keep ourselves spiritually strong is by harnessing our inner reserves of humanity, love and empathy, by praying, by reaching out, by connecting, by reading and sharing inspiring stories of compassion and altruism, by lending a helping hand, that is controlling what we can- faith in systems may be lost but we must not lose our faith in love, mercy and humanity because only this will keep hope afloat amidst the mire of gloom and despair.

Dr. Vineeta Kamran is the founder Principal at City Montessori School, Kanpur Road Branch, Lucknow

Life v/s Life Style

After staying at home with just family and virtual friends, like WhatsApp, Instagram, Facebook, Netflix, Youtube etc in this second wave of Covid, I realised a few aspects of life.

Spending time with the inert me, gave me "self realization". The Journey of life is very simple and we human beings make it complicated. It allowed me to think about things that I have achieved and where I have reached in this ladder of life.

The first realization leads me to the luxuries with what I have boosted my life with, my designation, my bank balance, my cars etc. The other realisation leads me to my overall development, what have I added to the society around me. The answers were quite diverse, my life till date was ruled by the unrealistic pressures around me. I had moved from just being me as an individual to the designation that I have on my visiting card. We as individuals are just running without giving any weightage to the journey leading to goals of life instead of spending time on what, why and when.

The pandemic apart from all the mayhem that it's creating is also giving us some time to introspect on the aspects of life that lured no importance in our day to day lives. It's pushing us to change our lifestyles from spending time in cinemas,malls on weekends to staying home, spending time with family. On the broader prospect it's pushing us to think about a cleaner and safer environment around us. Reduce the pollution levels in our urban areas and most importantly keep a check of our mental health. Every individual has a different way of taking care of their mental health. It varies from sleep, cook,binge watch to board games . Interestingly I found my mental health in inspirational stories of established and budding entrepreneurs and their journeys.

They were like life journeys portrayed in movies , but the difference being non- fictional. The emotions , the words used had a meaning of strength, stability and hardwork. Their journeys were commendable and some of them breathtaking.

Everything is within. Let's get into the cycle of 21 days to change ourselves.

When the outside situations go against us, we also turn against ourselves or we stand 100% keeping ourselves joyful, exuberant, alive. Let's be a part of the solution. We are all living in a box, we don't have contact with the five elements in nature. Viruses are changing our lifestyle. There is no need to complain, nothing has changed in Life, only our lifestyle has changed. We have misunderstood our lifestyle as life. How we live within ourselves is life. Life is precious instead of lifestyle. Let's accept the Change and be a Change for the Change.

Anuradhsri Anand is an extremely dynamic professional with over 25 years of hands-on experience in esteemed institutions India and overseas. She is a lifelong learner and believes in the principle of Action and Change and has a vast experience in setting up best of the K-12 schools, Pre schools (To name a few, PICT model School Pune, Credo World School Dahanu, Credo Joy Panvel and Nestling Pune) and daycares in the corporate world. She is a Director Principal, Group coordinator, Curriculum Planner, Early Childhood Educationist, Edupreneur, Multi Awardee, Trainer, Advisor, Mentor, Motivational Speaker and Quality Auditor and is based in Mumbai.

How to Stay Motivated in the COVID 19 pandemic?

It is quite normal for the body, mind to become overwhelmed, and exhausted with the negative psychological effects when our body systems are activating by the anxiety of the COVID19 pandemic trauma, which leads us tragedy to the chronic stress.

Currently, we are facing a chaos since we are operating with less structure in our life than usual due to the social isolation, few gatherings, less contacts with others than we normally do. Moreover, we are all facing additional stress due to the personal and family concerns such as political, economic, financial worries, and social concerns.

Definitely, all of this can make it hard to stay motivated. Yet, the big question is what we shall do in this current scenario! How can we set achievable goals, take care of ourselves, share positivity, and be hopeful?

It is quite challenging to feel more motivated in this situation. Yet, here are few suggestions that I would like to share with you to spark and maintain your motivation. We should start thinking together about our daily routine, wellbeing, academic routine, and the continuous professional development.

Let us start our day with a well-planned schedule: contact a close friend, break up our responsibilities down into manageable tasks, give ourselves encouraging rewards for speicfic tasks completed, and include few fun activities to your daily routine.

Next, moving to our wellbeing, try to keep yourself energized and take care of your wellbeing on daily basis: take breaks, go to the gym, follow a proper nutrition life style, stay on a regular sleep schedule, stay connected with positive peers, practice your favorite hobbies, and reach out for help when you need it without a single hesitation.

Third, the academic routine plays essential role to motivate ourselves. Accordingly, create a productive collaborative project, follow a schedule to complete your projects, use effective study strategies, study with your friends, join formal groups and communities, and keep in mind to reach out to your instructors for further support or clarifications.

Finally yet importantly, consider the continuous professional development as a daily priority. For example, prepare for future courses, sign up for online training, develop your professional skills, and enrich your personality to become a better citizenship that allows you to support your colleague, family, or your community.

The power of positivity thinking is the key for motivation. Like it or not, the COVID-19 pandemic has forced everyone to make changes accommodating with the new norms. Staying motivated can be tricky, but you can make it easier by few simple strategies. Though COVID19 pandemic feels endless, it will eventually end. Yet, it is your choice to make this end. Take a step forward and adopt now the motivation tips that can lead to positive and definite change for the rest of your life!

Farah Rustom is from Lebanon, she is an International Academician and has an extensive experience in administrative and HR management with a Master Degree in Educational Management and teaching background as a computing specialist in national & international UAE schools since 2002. Her recent managerial positions in Vantisco Youth Education Center, Italy allowed her to acquire a piece of wide knowledge of operations, coordination, and presentation techniques, in addition to developing her interpersonal and communication skills.

A Long Spell of Pandemic-What Kept Me Going?

First, let's ponder- the most remarkable scientific invention-atomic power assailed as the punishing invention that ruined generations. Unfortunately, Global warming is also a human invention, deadlier than the atomic catastrophe, but we are in denial. The COVID-19 pandemic may or may not be caused by humans, but it teaches us lessons in "Being Human."

Like the virus, "being human" is also mutating. The self-centred, self-aggrandising individuals suffering "VishwaRoopa" – larger than life-syndrome now believe that there is out there a force governing the universe. As a minuscule creation of God, I am no exception to this complex but soon realised and did a course correction. Surrender all you have, count your blessings and accept the impermanency became the mantra of the new toolkit.

The new survival playbook suddenly found the value in self-care, dating the self and finding solace in solitude, contemplation and regulating breathing. It was a part forced but largely embraced that intake of the junk food, daily doses of contaminated information- in the words of the WHO official-Infodemic, overdoses of polluted air, thoughts and practices reduced to the minimum.

The survival instinct of early 2020 metamorphosed to reconstruction, new learning, adaptation to remote interaction, resilience building and bringing in our armoury new tools of teaching, learning, sharing and collaborating and leading by example. Technology, with all its inadequacies and inaccessibility, proved the mythological "Sanjeevani." Amazing colleagues, friends and family chipping in with socio-emotional bondages filled the gaps created by the isolation, social distancing and home sheltering.

The pandemic brought the world communities together like never before without travelling an inch, saving tons of carbon footprint, no jet lags, experts from around the world obliged each other- beating all time zones. A hand folded "Namaste" replaced in one stroke all time-specific salutations the English language teaches. A 13" laptop screen became a permanent host to the guests serving coffee, breakfast, lunch or dinner as they chose in their standard time zones.

But for a teacher, the greatest gift during the pandemic is the company of students. Almost overnight, we realised for the first time that they are friends, collaborators, reverse mentors. Years of "Gyan" by the voluminous books, scholarly writings and learned teachings of the philosophers could not teach us the value of respecting the students' potential. Still, the pandemic cast a magical spell of change. I am amazed by the resilience of the students, their creativity and their ability to initiate change. Of course, the second wave of the pandemic has been more challenging. Even the bravest get toppled in the wake of managing death in the family.

My wife and I are both teachers. As a storyteller, she engaged children in the age group 4 to 8, listening to them, observing their behaviour and innocence. I engaged with the older ones driving them to come out, open up and form self-help groups. I cannot discount the critical role books played-10 of them I read- during these trying times. Coincidently or by God's design, the one in my hand now is "The Unthinkable Earth"-A story of the future- by David Wallace-Wells.

Ashok Pandey is a Delhi based Educationist and National Coordinator, Climate Education- Climate Reality Project India.

Pandemic *is one of the most important difficult times within the history of humankind. We have been living with all the serious health and social problems of Covid-19 virus since the beginning of the year 2020. However, it is* *our responsibility to be resilient and problem solver to keep the psychology of our kids in equilibrium. Life necessitates being healthy in terms of physical an, mental and emotional health as well.*

In addition to the huge responsibility of authorities of the States, every person is obliged to be helpful to the people around him/her. Educators must be horror-busters giving joy and calmness to their students to remove the barriers of Covid-19 on them. Congratulations for your hard work and commitment to educational development of kids.

Assoc. Prof. Dr. Hayal KÖKSAL, Academician, Quality & Peace Expert, Author, NGO Leader, Founding President, Association for Innovative Collaboration (YİMEDER), Director General (TR), World Council for Total Quality &Excellence in Education (WCTQEE), Advisor of Istanbul AIESEC & Designer-General Coordinator of ICT Seagulls Projects, Turkey.

Keeping yourself motivated even during the current scenario"

This is the best time and the worst time The Tales of Two Cities

What does the VUCA Mean ? There are many phrases to describe the critical time , especial the term −New Normal! But until Dr. M told me about the VUCA had I found the most absolutely term to express ourselves, and these guidelines would help adjust ourselves in the VUCA time. The first organizations to use the VUCA acronym was the United States Army War College was one of them. Following the 9/ 11 terrorist attacks in 2001. Military planners were worried about the radically different and unfamiliar international security environment that had emerged, so they used VUCA to describe it.

VUCA stands for:

Volatile − change is rapid and unexpected in its nature and extent.

Uncertain − the present is unclear and the future is uncertain.

Complex − many different, interconnected factors with the potential to cause chaos and confusion.

Ambiguous – there is a lack of clarity or awareness about situations.

What Have I learned and transformed?

We are forced to adjust ourselves to a certain way. Let me share my story how I have adjusted myself and learned in this VUCA time. I am an English teacher in Taiwan and I have been teaching English with 20 years of experiences. As an educator, you need to learn before you teach. Teaching is an emotional journey which takes emotional labor.

Happiness counts- Happy teachers make happy students, and happy students make successful learning. Now the learners are learning at home, facing isolation, stress due to individual's social status. Even there are not a few facing no learning internet access. If they do , put their emotional needs before my academic goals.

Developing Autonomous Learners

Teachers will not be the sole resources of knowledge. With the technology and internet access, the learners could learn anytime, anywhere with boarders. We definitely need to prepare our learners to be equipped with digital literacy. With the right mindset in mind, the learners could gain all kinds of knowledge through the digital world, they would learn based on their critical thinking skill and mind.

Reimagining Teacher's Role

Teaching is learning. We are in the constantly changing world, we need to activate ourselves to be a ife long learner as well. In the pandemic VUCA World in particular., this book shared the approach with understanding the notion in Visualising the learning in a big way. It integrates about the model to manage the world through VOCA in the COVID era. Reading the book is like having yourselves in the breeze . These insights will train us to manage through the Volatility, Uncertainty, Complexity, Ambiguity, as VOCA in practice.

Ming Yao Hsiung is an English Teacher with 20 years of teaching experience from Taipei Wanfu Public Elementary School, Taiwan. She is also the Director of Taipei Wanfu English Teaching and Learning Center, Google Certified Educator and a Microsoft Innovative Educator from Taiwan.

Keeping yourself and your team motivated even during the current scenario

Two men looked out of the prison bar One saw the mud and the other the star...

Yes this is very true that it is the mind set which matters during the crisis like we all are facing these days. On 22nd March 2020 we all got closed within the four walls of our houses along with our children and our teams. We were in a dilemma as to how to handle the crisis which had come uninformed and suddenly. We all within no time went online with our studies. Many leaders crossed the first hurdles of moving their teams remote via Zoom, Google Meet, MS Teams etc. within no time and ensured that all their colleagues had set up their tech tools, defined their processes as to how to go ahead with the virtual classes, and permanently logged into their video conference accounts. But this is just the first step towards creating an effective work environment for remote employees but the most critical question was how to keep them motivated throughout. It indeed was a million dollar question how to keep ourselves motivated during this difficult time. The matrix of life is woven with the warp and weft of the bright and dull colours and we need to balance between the two in a very Superpositive way. It is said that every cloud has a silver lining and every night has a day to follow and every winter will be followed by the spring. It is the positivity which promises us an *oasis in the desert, a dawn in the darkness and light at end of a tunnel. It is well said that life is 10% what happens to us and 90% of how we react to it. It is the positive mindset that gives us choice to play the tune of our choice even when we cannot change the musical instrument gifted to us.*

Covid 19 pandemic has made life challenging in ways , work, socialize , the loss of jobs, men and material coupled with uncertainty has thrown life out of control. The entire mankind is going through a tough time and there is overwhelming despair and depression around. While we know it is helpful for everyone to stay superpositive, it is not easy when unpleasant accidents overwhelm our mind. But here are some powerful suggestions for self-growth and empowerments to transform our outlook.

Always remember " Tough times never last but tough people do." This time too shall pass. Trials will be transformed into triumphs if we utilize this time for self growth and empowerment. Life is not mere existence but a journey of self-improvement. Toddlers, take a baby step, hop, or jump but never stop. If you happen to find yourself with spare time, here are some ways we get engaged constructively as we did at DPSG Vasundhara :

We ensured that we have a Yoga and sports session Virtually too in our curriculum to keep the staff and students engaged with a superpositive state of mind.

Learn to meditate for meditation clears the cloud of negativity and renders our mind clean again like sky.

Learn a new language or a new instrument or take an online course to enhance your acumen.

Using You Tube to learn and share your learning with others.

Practice gratefulness for a millions are not able to wake up in the morning to enjoy the company of their loved ones.

Chanting the Superpositivty Mantra " Yes Thank You Universe" had kept me superbly charged even during the Covid times.

Never forget to exercise as that releases the endorphins in your body, which trigger feelings of positivity, so be sure to include an exercise routine in your day, even if it is only a short one. The regular dose of exercise is better than the single overdose.

We can learn to sing, dance or have the family time and understand each other better.

I involved myself in social services where I could help providing the food to the Covid Patients and their Families and that gave such a sense of satisfaction by helping humanity which cannot be expressed in words. I got the Oxygen First Aid and the Isolation Centre set up in my school DPSGV which was a real help to the people who did not get beds in hospitals from 5th April 2021 to 21st May 2021. I think this kind of supperpositive involvement made me feel like giving back to the society. I was also involved in a lot of CBSE Workshops, IPN Workshops, Sessions for EduTV and a lot of session to train the teachers from Arunanchal Pradesh, Jammu and Kashmir, Khatima, Maharasthra, Bhopal schools and a lot of South Indian Schools.

In the bargain I did not find the time to crib and lament on the situation posed by Covid 19. I utilized this time to explore , know, understand the IB PYP curriculum and get it started in our School which really widen up my *horizon. Before I sum up, I will say " Stay Calm and Constructive in times of adversity as it will help us navigate through difficulties and find a path towards healthier, happier and richer life."*

Trilok Singh Bist is a Principal at Delhi Public School Ghaziabad, Vasundhara, in Delhi NCR

One wonders *what anyone can learn during a Pandemic?! These are times when fear runs amok, and we have to practice constraint in all walks of life. From economy to entertainment to travel everything has been brought down on its knees. The human development has been stifled beyond repair. Every home is has a story of grief,despair and loss. Is there anything which can be viewed in a positive light during such dark times?*

As Pandemics are bound to strike every 100 years, we need to understand what repercussions the previous ones had on our lives. E.g. When the London plague happened the city dwellers decided to restructure, revamp and reorganize their city spaces. Making it cleaner, greener and sewage and drainage system was revamped. So the important question to ask would be, have we learnt any lessons? First and foremost, we realized that there are numerous jobs which did not need the investment it received. Take for example, office spaces. The majority of the employees in IT sector for example, continue to do their jobs from the confines of their homes. Huge expensive office spaces and cramped residential area with expensive rentals can now be foregone. We also understood how ill equipped we are in our health sector, to handle an over load of patients. We could have easily invested in Health care and emergency equipment's, but it was clearly a case of over sight and bad planning. With medicines being sold for five times their cost, the authorities have been powerless and disabled in the hands of the game of demand and supply, with corruption seen everywhere from health care to pharmacy and allied services.

Ironically, Education has seen its own downfall in some parts and upliftment in other areas. The thrust to digitalise education happened like never before. However despite the hype about Online education, we haven't been able to give equitable online education to even 55 percent of our student population. This leaves us with a huge gap in learning. To compensate it will take years. Hence, we must bring a digital revolution in our Tier B and C cities and help organize our Internet service providers. This monopoly of Internet services which is in the hands of a few capitalists must be nationalized because quality education is the birth right of every citizen of India!

Pooja Bose is a Principal at the The High range School, Munnar, Kerala

About The Author

Dr Dheeraj Mehrotra is an Author, Teacher Trainer, School Auditor, A National Teacher Awardee, engaged as a Principal at Kunwar's Global School, Lucknow, India. He has authored over 100 plus books on various topics and has also been listed in the LIMCA Book of Records and INDIA Book of Records for his innovation in Education. As a TEDx speaker and as a premium UDEMY Instructor he has also developed over 400 Courses and believes in learning to learn as a priority.

ABOUT THE AUTHOR

He can be visited at
www.authordheerajmehrotra.com

Books By The Same Author

www.authordheerajmehrotra.com

www.ingramcontent.com/pod-product-compliance
Lightning Source LLC
Chambersburg PA
CBHW050340160726
48002CB00001B/395